BASIC MUSIC

An Activities Approach
to Functional Musicianship

THIRD EDITION

PRENTICE-HALL INTERNATIONAL, INC., *London*
PRENTICE-HALL OF AUSTRALIA, PTY. LTD., *Sydney*
PRENTICE-HALL OF CANADA, LTD., *Toronto*
PRENTICE-HALL OF INDIA (PRIVATE) LTD., *New Delhi*
PRENTICE-HALL OF JAPAN, INC., *Tokyo*

BASIC MUSIC

An Activities Approach
to Functional Musicianship

THIRD EDITION

Robert E. Nye
Professor of Music
University of Oregon

Bjornar Bergethon
Professor of Music
University of Illinois

ILLINOIS CENTRAL COLLEGE
LEARNING RESOURCE CENTER

PRENTICE-HALL, INC., Englewood Cliffs, New Jersey

33151

© 1968 by PRENTICE-HALL, INC., Englewood Cliffs, New Jersey
(Previously copyrighted © 1954, 1962 under the title, BASIC MUSIC FOR
CLASSROOM TEACHERS)

Library of Congress Catalog Card No.: 68-11290

Current printing (last digit):

10 9 8 7 6 5 4 3

Preface

The purpose of this book is to assist the classroom teacher in acquiring the basic musicianship needed to teach music effectively in the elementary school. The activities suggested represent an integrated approach to the elements of music through singing and listening, playing instruments, reading and writing musical notation, analyzing and creating music. The emphasis is on *making music*. Starting with the singing and playing of easy, familiar songs, the student continues to make music in a variety of ways, gaining in musical comprehension and skill through a series of activities which are carefully graded with regard to difficulty.

Basic concepts of rhythm, melody, harmony, and form are dealt with from the very beginning in a functional manner. Musical terminology and theoretical details are introduced gradually and specifically only as needed, the approach being experience first, explanation later. In this way these aspects of musicianship are learned easily and efficiently because they apply directly to the music at hand, and therefore make sense.

This edition has been expanded to include chapters dealing with *Intervals, Scales, and Chords, Expressive Singing, The Pentatonic Scale and the Modes, Concepts of Musical Form, Style Periods in Music* and *Instruments and Voices*. Many new songs and a repertoire of listening selections have also been added. Other new features are specific chapter assignments for *Developing Skills* and *Analytic-Creative Activities* for independent study and reenforcement of musical learnings.

The Authors

Contents

BASIC MUSIC

An Activities Approach to Functional Musicianship

THIRD EDITION

1

Rhythm, Melody, Harmony, and Form

Let us begin our study of basic music by focusing attention on four concepts of musical organization: rhythm, melody, harmony, and form. Through singing and playing a few well-known songs we shall discover how rhythm and melody are interrelated, how they are shaped into formal designs, and how harmony can be used to support the rhythmic structure and add color to the melodic line. At the same time, we shall be developing increasing skill in singing and in playing instruments, in listening to music, and in reading music notation.

RHYTHM AND MELODY

Sing the following familiar songs in a manner appropriate to the meaning of the words.

LOVE SOMEBODY

2. Love somebody, can't guess who,
   Love somebody, but I won't tell who.

3. Love somebody's eyes of blue,
   Love somebody, but I won't tell who.

4. Love somebody's smile so true,
   Love somebody, but I won't tell who.

DEAF WOMAN'S COURTSHIP

Moderately

Southern Mountain Song

Old wo-man, old wo-man, are you fond of spin-ning?

Speak a lit-tle loud-er, sir, I'm ver-y hard of hear-ing.

2. Old woman, old woman, will you do my mending?
   Speak a little louder, sir, I'm very hard of hearing.

3. Old woman, old woman, are you fond of cooking?
   Speak a little louder, sir, I'm very hard of hearing.

4. Old woman, old woman, will you let me court you?
   Speak a little louder, sir, I just begin to hear you.

5. Old woman, old woman, would you like to marry me?
   O my goodness, gracious sake, I think that now I hear you.

Rhythm of the Beat. Sing these songs several times and clap your hands in time to the music. You will notice that there is a steady *beat* or *pulse* which continues uninterrupted throughout the song regardless of whether the tones of the melody are longer or shorter. As you continue to sing and to clap you will observe that the beats fall into a pattern which you can count as "ONE-Two," "ONE-Two," the first being heavy (*accented*) and the second light (*unaccented*).

Old wo-man, old wo-man, are you fond of spin-ning?

>   >   >   >

1   2   1   2   1   2   1   2

(>) *accent marking*

Emphasize this distinction between the two beats by clapping louder on the accented beat.

Now conduct the songs as you sing by moving your right hand *down* on

2

the accented beat and *up* on the unaccented beat, like this:

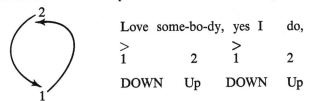

Love	some-bo-dy,	yes I	do,
>		>	
1	2	1	2
DOWN	Up	DOWN	Up

The first beat, "ONE," is called the *down-beat* and the second beat, "TWO," is called the *up-beat*.

"Go Tell Aunt Rhody" is another song which moves in twos, although at a somewhat slower pace or *tempo*. Notice in conducting this song that your hand and arm will move slower to accommodate the difference in tempo between this and "Love Somebody."

GO TELL AUNT RHODY

2. The one she's been saving . . . . . . to make a feather bed,
3. She died in the mill pond . . . . . . a-standing on her head.
4. The old gander's weeping . . . . . . because his wife is dead.
5. The goslings are weeping . . . . . . because their mother's dead,

Rhythm of the Melody. Next, sing "Go Tell Aunt Rhody" paying particular attention to how the melody moves in relation to the beat as you tap this lightly with your hand or foot. You will notice that not all the tones of the melody fall on the beat: some occur on the beat, others come between beats, and the last note is sustained longer than one beat. The *rhythm of the melody*, therefore, is quite different from the rhythm of the beat because some syllables are sung on short tones while others are sung on longer tones. As you sing the song again, observe that the *melody-rhythm* coincides with the *word-rhythm*.

The rhythm of the melody is sometimes symbolized in *line-notation*, which serves as a visual aid to observing the rhythmic features of the melody, i.e. the relative *duration* of the tones within the melody. The melody-rhythm for "Go Tell Aunt Rhody" would look like this in line-notation:

— — — — — — — — — — —

— — — — — — — — — —

Clap this rhythm while counting the beats, "ONE-Two."

In order to indicate the accent of the first beat we draw a vertical line into the line notation, thus:

$$\left|\;\overline{}\;\overline{}\;\underline{}\;\right|\;\overline{}\;\overline{}\;\underline{}\;\left|\;\overline{}\;\overline{}\;\underline{}\;\right|\;\underline{}\;\underline{}\;\overline{}$$

$$\quad 1 \qquad 2 \qquad 1 \qquad 2 \qquad 1 \qquad 2 \qquad 1 \qquad 2$$

Observe that this line is drawn to the *left* of the line-note on which the accent falls. Insert this vertical line into the other half of the line-notation above for "Go Tell Aunt Rhody"; then clap the melody-rhythm again, accenting the first beat as you count.

The steady beat or pulse is the regulator of the rhythmic movement of the melody. However, every melody has its own rhythmic pattern which becomes a characteristic of that particular melody. Discover this for yourself by comparing the melody-rhythms of "Go Tell Aunt Rhody" and "Deaf Woman's Courtship." Write down the line notation of the latter, in the space provided, for comparison.

Symbols for Duration. Since music is "sound in time," we must have some way of indicating just how long each tone in a melody should be sustained. Line-notation can only indicate approximate *duration.* A more precise way of indicating the relative duration of tones within a melody is to use *notes* of different shapes. If you look at the printed notation for "Go Tell Aunt Rhody,"

you will see that it has three differently shaped notes: ♩, ♫, ♩.. As you sing the melody and clap the beats while looking at the notation, you

will discover that the first kind of note (♩), called *quarter note,* coincides

with the beat while it takes two notes of the second kind (♫), called *eighth notes,* to equal the duration of a beat, and that the third kind of note

(♩), called *half note,* has a duration of two beats. From this you can see that there is a 1 to 2 relationship between these *note values,* or note durations, which can be expressed as follows:

$$\text{♩} \;=\; \text{♫} \qquad\qquad \text{♩} \;=\; \text{♩ ♩}$$

4

This relative duration of note values is one of the basic concepts of rhythmic notation which we shall explore further in Chapter 2. For the present, look at the notation again and reinforce your understanding of this concept by clapping the melody-rhythm and tapping the beat rhythm with your foot as you count "ONE-Two," "ONE-Two." Do the same with "Deaf Woman's Courtship" and the following familiar song, "Lightly Row."

LIGHTLY ROW

With gentle motion

German Folk Song

Light - ly row, light - ly row, o'er the glas - sy waves we go;

Smooth - ly glide, Smooth - ly glide, on the si - lent tide.

Let the winds and wa - ters be min - gled with our mel - o - dy;

Sing and float, sing and float, in our lit - tle boat.

MELODY AND FORM

As you sing and listen to "Lightly Row," you sense that the melody moves forward toward the tone for the word "go," where it seems to come to a momentary pause; and then, it progresses until it reaches the word "tide," where there is a longer pause. Such pauses in the melody are called *cadences*, and a cadence marks the end of a musical *phrase*. A phrase may be likened to a musical comment or thought; cadences act as musical punctuation marks to conclude phrases. In songs, phrases often correspond to the lines of the poetry. Thus there are four phrases in "Lightly Row."

1. Lightly row, lightly row, o'er the glassy waves we go;

2. Smoothly glide, smoothly glide, on the silent tide.

3. Let the winds and waters be mingled with our melody;

4. Sing and float, sing and float, in our little boat.

Listen to the separate phrases. Can you hear that three of them are almost alike? Which one is different from the others? How do the four phrases differ from each other? If you can hear such similarities and differences in the phrase structure of music, you have sensed the essence of *form* in music. Form embodies *unity* and *variety;* unity can be represented by repetition of like or near-like phrases; variety can be supplied by contrasting phrases.

The arrangement of the phrases in "Lightly Row" is called a *three-part song form* or an *ABA* form. (While AABA would be a more accurate description of this form, it is customary to use ABA as its abbreviation.) "Go Tell Aunt Rhody" is an example of the *two-part song form* or *AB* form. What is the essential difference between these two forms?

An awareness of form is especially helpful in learning and memorizing new songs; it is also useful in many other musical activities, as you will find in succeeding chapters.

MELODIC MOVEMENT

The melody of "Whistle, Daughter, Whistle" consists of one single phrase and its repetition.

WHISTLE, DAUGHTER, WHISTLE

With mock seriousness   American Folk Song

Mother
Whis- tle, Daugh- ter, whis - tle, and you shall have a cow.

Daughter
I can't whis - tle, Moth - er, You nev - er taught me how.

2. Whistle, Daughter, whistle, and you shall have a goat.
   I can't whistle, Mother, because it hurts my throat.

3. Whistle, Daughter, whistle, and you shall have a pig.
   I can't whistle, Mother, because I am too big.

4. Whistle, Daughter, whistle, and you shall have a man.
   (whistle   ), I'll do the best I can.

A melody is a succession of tones, or *pitches,* the movement of which is governed by rhythm. Pitch is a term which refers to the relative highness or lowness of a tone. As you listen to the melody of "Whistle, Daughter, Whistle," your ear will tell you that the tones move in three ways, upward, downward, or stay on the same level, like this:

Whis - tle,   Daugh - ter,   whis - tle,   and   you   shall   have   a   cow.

Tonal movement and direction are important concepts of melodic organization that should be emphasized in early musical experiences.

Melodic movement can be visualized in various ways. One way of doing this is to use hand motions to show how successive tones sound higher or lower or stay in the same place. As you sing the melody hold your hand in front of you, palm down, and raise or lower the hand to match the relative height of the tones. Another way is to use line-notation to represent these *pitch levels,* as well as their duration. The line-notation for "Whistle, Daughter Whistle" would look like this:

Practice singing this melody on a neutral syllable such as "loo," with hand motions. Next, act out the melodic direction with your hand silently; close your eyes and *think* the melody apart from any sounds. Do this several times until you truly feel the pitch levels of the separate tones in the melody. Do the same with other songs.

PITCH NOTATION

Line-notation as a device for indicating the exact pitches of a melody has its limitations. For a more precise method of doing this we must use the conventional notation system which employs notes in combination with a *music staff.* We have already observed how different kinds of notes may be used to symbolize the relative duration of the tones in a melody. These same notes can also be used as symbols for exact pitches when they are placed on a music staff.

The staff consists of five lines and four spaces which are numbered from the bottom and upward:

7

Each line and each space has its own *pitch name* derived from the musical "alphabet" which employs only seven letters: A B C D E F G. These can be visualized on a piano keyboard:

PIANO KEYBOARD

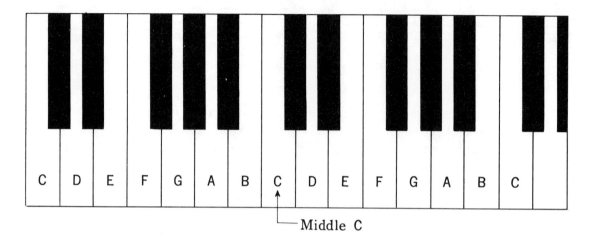

As you look at this keyboard you will see that the white and black keys are arranged so that the black keys fall into groups of twos and threes. The white key to the left of the two black keys is C and the key by that name in the center of the keyboard is called *middle C*. We shall refer to this key again as we continue our explanation of pitch notation.

The pitch names for the lines and spaces are determined by a *clef sign* which is placed at the beginning of the staff. The two most commonly used clefs are the *treble clef* (𝄞) and the *bass clef* (𝄢). The treble clef is also called the *G clef* because it designates the pitch name for the *second* line of the staff as "G" above middle C.

Using this clef as a point of orientation we can now name the lines and spaces of the treble staff:

The treble staff is used to notate music which is intended for relatively high-pitched voices and instruments: children's and women's voices, flute, oboe, clarinet, saxophone, trumpet, French horn, and violin.

The bass clef is also called the *F clef* because it designates the pitch name for the *fourth* line of the staff as "F" below middle C.

The names of the lines and spaces of the *bass staff* are:

The bass staff is used primarily for music intended for lower-pitched voices and instruments: men's voices, bassoon, trombone, baritone, tuba, cello, string bass, and tympani.

Short lines, called *leger lines,* are added above or below the staff in order to accommodate pitches which are higher or lower than those which can be

9

notated within the staff itself. Thus, middle C is on the first leger line below the treble staff and on the first leger line above the bass staff.

When the treble and bass staffs are used together, they form a *grand staff* of eleven lines with the middle C leger line in the center.

THE GRAND STAFF

The grand staff is used for music written for the piano, organ, harp, and celeste.

Reading Pitch Notation. Teachers use different approaches for introducing children to the reading of pitch notation. Some will use the letter names of the pitches (A, B, C, D, E, F, G); others may use number names (1, 2, 3, 4, 5, 6, 7, 8) or syllable names (*do, re, mi, fa, so, la, ti, do*); many use all three approaches. Whichever names are used, they will most often be related to a scale pattern, usually the familiar *major* scale.[1] Sing this scale ascending and descending in all three ways:

THE C SCALE

C	D	E	F	G	A	B	C		C	B	A	G	F	E	D	C
1	2	3	4	5	6	7	8		8	7	6	5	4	3	2	1
do	re	mi	fa	so	la	ti	do		do	ti	la	so	fa	mi	re	do

This is called the scale of C because it begins and ends on C.

[1] Scales and their construction will be discussed in Chapter 3.

If you look at the notation of the songs in this chapter, you will see that all the tones in the melodies belong to this C scale; therefore, we say that these songs are in the *key of C*.

Singing with Numbers and Syllables. The first two phrases of "Lightly Row" would be sung like this with number names:

Phrase 1:   5 3 3__ 4 2 2__ 1 2 3 4 5 5 5__

Phrase 2:   5 3 3__ 4 2 2__ 1 3 5 5 3_____

Phrase 3:

Phrase 4:

With syllable names they would be sung like this: [2]

Phrase 1:   s m m__ f r r__ d r m f s s s__

Phrase 2:   s m m__ f r r__ d m s s m_____

Phrase 3:

Phrase 4:

Write down the remaining phrases in the same manner and sing "Lightly Row" in both ways with hand motions.

SINGING

Many people are fortunate in that they have had a great deal of experience in singing, enjoy it, and are confident about it. Others may have to work to remedy deficiencies in their childhood education which have left them with a few problems in the use of their voices.

Occasionally a person may not have been helped to listen carefully to pitches and pitch changes. As we know, pitches can repeat, move up, or move down. Sometimes they move stepwise and sometimes they move by skips. By listening carefully to these aspects of pitch, and by playing familiar songs on bells or piano, individuals can help themselves to improved hearing. With practice in playing such songs on these keyboard instruments they can eventually sing the pitches they play and can feel the distance between pitches as they play them. Later they can sing the songs without the aid of an instrument.

Sometimes the major difficulty is the voice range. The songs thus far have been placed in the easiest range for beginning group singing, and performing them should be no problem for anyone. However, songs later on in this book will have a wider range. If some of these seem "too high," the singer may be using only the lower part of his natural range, the "chest voice," and needs to discover and learn to use the higher part of his natural range, the "head voice." Students who have never used this higher voice may quite properly find themselves sounding like young children's singing until there has been time to develop this new voice. *Those who already know their voices are "too low" should begin now to find and develop the head voice* in order

[2] The single letter for the syllable names is a "shorthand" method used in many European countries.

to be able to utilize their full vocal range. The way to begin is to imitate the voice of the young child, as suggested above.

The voice quality most pleasing is a natural-sounding one in which there is no evidence of strain or discomfort. There will be breath support to sustain the tone. Voice quality will vary to some extent in accordance with the meaning of the words of songs. For example, the type of tone desirable in a lullaby would be different than the tone desired in a stirring patriotic song. A relaxed throat is always recommended. Teachers commonly ask for "an open, relaxed mouth and throat."

The musical phrase should not be broken by taking a breath; the singer plans for sufficient breath to complete the phrase. Of course words should never be broken by attempting to take a breath between syllables. Often the punctuation gives the singer direction as to where to breathe; usually one sings as he speaks, with regard to breathing. Tones are *attacked* and *released* in accordance with the notated music. It helps to remember that singing is only sustained speech; we sing vowels and sustain them; usually consonants are only a form of punctuation separating the vowels.

PLAYING MELODIES

Various types of simple melody instruments may be used to help reinforce aural concepts of melodic organization and to further the ability to read music notation. Of the many instruments available for classroom use we have chosen the *Resonator Bells*[3] and the *piano* for our purpose.

Resonator Bells. Courtesy Ludwig Drum Co.

A unique feature of the Resonator Bells is that the tonebars are mounted separately so that the player can choose whichever ones are needed for any given purpose.

Note that the white and black bars are arranged like the piano keyboard and that the names of the pitches are stamped into the metal bars. This makes it easy to select those needed to play a particular melody. The songs

[3] Mallet-played instruments of various types are available in many sizes and price ranges. Some of the more popular instruments are the *Step Bells*, the *Song Bells* or *Tone Bells*, and the *xylophone*.

we have been singing in this chapter utilized only the following pitches: C D E F G. Remove these bars from the case and arrange them in order from *low* to *high* pitches, like this:

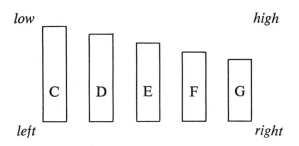

As you play the melodies on these bells you will become aware of an important concept concerning keyboard-type instruments: that tones which go "up" are played by moving to the *right* and that tones which go "down" are played by moving to the *left*.

It is very easy to play these same melodies on the piano. Find middle C and place the thumb of your right hand on this key; then play the tones C D E F G successively with the five fingers this way:

You should have no difficulty in playing the melodies on the piano if you keep your hand in this five-finger position.

If you would like to play the melodies with the left hand, you should place the little finger of this hand on C in order to be in a convenient five-finger position. Choosing the C below middle C for the left hand makes it possible to play the melodies with both hands together. Try this.

PLAYING ACCOMPANIMENTS

Accompaniments add interest and color to the singing and playing of songs. One very effective, yet simple, type of accompaniment which is used frequently is called "chording." A *chord* is a combination of two or more tones sounded together. Chords produce *harmony*, and a succession of chords creates *harmonic movement*. Harmony gives coloristic support to the melody and reinforces the rhythmic movement as well. The Autoharp [4] and the piano are both suitable for chording.[5]

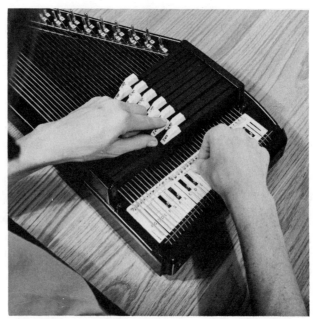

Autoharp. Courtesy Oscar-Schmidt International, Inc.

Autoharp Chording. Place the Autoharp on a table or desk or in your lap so that the corner of the two straight sides points toward the body. With the left-hand index finger firmly press down the button marked "C Maj," and stroke the strings from left to right with the right hand, using a hard felt or celluloid pick. The stroke should cover the full range of strings. Next, press the button marked "G₇" with the middle finger and stroke, or strum, the strings as before. Practice pressing the buttons and strumming, alternately, until you can change from one *chord* to another easily. In doing so, familiarize yourself with the sound of each chord.

You now have two chords which can be used for creating accompaniments to the songs you have been singing and playing. Look at the notation for these songs and you will see that the chords to be used are indicated above the staff. Different people will have different ideas here, but most of you will strum on the same beats you clapped a while ago; others may want to chord only on "ONE" and rest on "two."

Chord Names. Chords receive their names from the tones of the scale upon which they are built. All the melodies you have sung and played in this chapter are in the key of C. The Autoharp chords that you used to accompany these songs also belong to the key of C. The first chord, "C," is called *C chord* or *I chord* because it is built on the first degree of the C scale. The second chord is called *G₇ chord* or *V₇ chord* because it is built on the fifth degree of the scale. The lowest tone of such chord is called the *chord root,* and

[4] The Autoharp comes in various sizes: 5-bar, 12-bar, and 15-bar. The latter two are recommended.

[5] Other chording instruments are the ukulele and the guitar.

14

therefore the chord receives its name from its *root,* the pitch name or number of the scale tone on which it is built.

The I chord is also called *tonic chord* because its chord root is the *tonic* or 1 of the scale. The fifth step of the scale is called *dominant* and therefore the V₇ chord also goes by the name of *dominant seventh chord.*

Piano Chording. Chording can be done in several ways on the piano. One would be to play the chords as notated above with the right hand. The three tones of the I chord could be played in the five-finger position you used for playing the melodies. For the V₇ chord you would have to place the thumb on G and then play the other notes with index, ring, and little fingers. If you were to play these chords with the left hand, they would probably be notated in the bass clef, like this:

Find these chords on the piano keyboard.

In trying to play the chords as notated above you probably discovered that you have had to move your hands a great deal. However, there is a much easier way to play the I-V₇ progression which will enable you to add piano accompaniments to songs much more readily. For the present we shall limit ourselves to chording with the left hand only.

Place the little finger of your left hand on the C-key below middle C, the middle finger on the E-key, and the thumb on the G-key. When you play these three keys simultaneously, you are playing the C chord.

THE C CHORD

The G_7 chord is played from the C-E-G position in the following manner: move the little finger down to the B-key; place the index finger on the F-key; and leave the thumb on the G-key, as before. Playing the B-F-G together produces the G_7 chord.[6]

THE G⁷ CHORD

Practice playing these two chords alternately until you get the feel of the chord changes. After you have achieved some facility in doing this, you will be able to play all the songs in this chapter with the melody in the right hand together with the accompaniment in the left hand without much difficulty.

DEVELOPING SKILLS

SINGING

1. Practice singing the songs with words, giving special attention to good diction, proper phrasing, and appropriate voice quality.

2. Practice singing the melodies with numbers and syllables while acting out the pitch levels with hand motions.

PLAYING

1. Practice playing the melodies on bells and piano.

2. Practice playing the C and the G_7 chords on the piano and Autoharp.

3. Practice playing the melodies and the chords together on the piano.

---

[6] Note that the fourth tone of the G_7 chord, D, has been left out; this can be done without altering the quality of this chord. A more detailed discussion of the I and V_7 chords will be given in Chapter 3.

READING

1. Practice naming the following pitches:

2. Practice singing the following tonal sequences with letter names, numbers, and syllables:

3. Practice clapping the following rhythmic phrases:

4. Make up groups of players and perform two or more of the above rhythmic phrases together as *duets, trios,* or *quartets.* Use different instruments for each part (drums, sticks, woodblock, triangle, etc.).

WRITING

1. Practice drawing treble and bass clef signs.

2. Practice writing the notes found in the songs (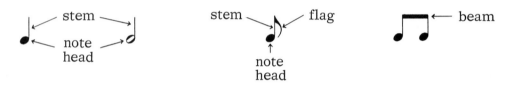) and placing them on the staff, using the following rules as guides:

   a. Notes have the following properties: *note head* ("black" or "open"), *stem,* and *flag.* When flags are joined together, they are called *beams.*

   b. Note heads are placed on the lines or in the spaces of the staff for the pitches desired.

   c. Stems may extend upward or downward. A note on the third line of the staff may have its stem either upward or downward:

   A note below this line has its stem extended upward and a note above this line has its stem extended downward.

   If the stem extends upward, it is placed to the right of the note; if it extends downward, it is placed to the left of the note; see above.

3. Complete writing the indicated pitches with the same kind of notes:

C   D   E   G   F   E   B   F   D   C   A   C   E   G   D

4. Complete transcribing the notation of "Go Tell Aunt Rhody" to the bass clef:

VOCABULARY

Practice defining or explaining the following musical terms:

accent	form	rhythm
beat	grand staff	staff
cadence	harmony	tempo
chord	key	tone
clef	leger line	tonic
conduct	melody	three-part form
dominant	note	two-part form
down-beat	phrase	up-beat
duration	pitch	

ANALYTIC-CREATIVE ACTIVITIES

1. Create several different rhythmic patterns based on ♩, ♩ and ♫ and present these to the class. Establish the underlying beat and have the class repeat the patterns like an "echo."

2. Experiment with "question and answer" clapping or drumming. One person may create (improvise) the question and another can be called upon to improvise an answer.

   Example:

3. On which tones of the scale of C do the melodies of the songs in this chapter begin and end? Are these tones related to the I chord? How?

4. Study the melodies to see in which direction they move. Is there a change of direction within a phrase? Do the phrases begin on the same tone of the scale? Are any tonal patterns within the phrases repeated?

5. Using the knowledge obtained through 3 and 4 above, create a melody phrase of your own based on the tones of the C chord (C, E, G). Use quarter, eighth, and half notes.

6. Using your knowledge of two-part form (see "Deaf Woman's Courtship" and "Go Tell Aunt Rhody"), create a two-part form melody using the five tones of the scale: C, D, E, F, and G.

7. Try this experiment. Divide the class into two equal groups. At the same time have one group sing "Deaf Woman's Courtship" and the other "Go Tell Aunt Rhody." Evaluate the result and explain it by analyzing the chord structure and melody structure of the songs.

(A)

(F)

(A) Tone block

(B) rhythm sticks

courtesy Peripole, Incorporated

(B)

(I)

(C)

(J)

(G)

(D)

(H)

(E)

(K)

(A) Triangle, (B) gong, (C) maracas, (D) drum, (E) claves, (F) finger cymbals, (G) conga drum, (H) guiro, (I) bongo drums, (J) tambourine, (K) drum. *Photograph courtesy Tommy Moore, President, Rhythm Band, Incorporated, P.O. Box 126, Fort Worth, Texas.*

Musical Meter and Rhythmic Notation

Most of the music you are likely to come into contact with gives the impression of moving in accent groupings of twos or threes; that is, you can count "ONE-Two" or "ONE-Two-Three" as you listen to or perform the music. The songs in the previous chapter afforded you experience with "two-beat" rhythm. Here are two songs exemplifying "three-beat" rhythm.

DU, DU LIEGST MIR IM HERZEN

German

Du,   du   liegst   mir   im   Herz - en,
You,   you   live   in   my   heart,_____

Du,   du   liegst   mir   im   Sinn,
You,   you,   live   in   my   mind,

Du,   du   machst   mir   viel   Schmerz - en,
You,   you,   make   me   feel   sad,_____

Weisst   nicht,   wie   gut   ich   dir   bin?_____
Do   you   not   know   I   love   you?_____

[1] The numbers over the notes are suggested fingerings for playing the melody on the piano: 1—thumb, 2—index finger, 3—middle finger, 4—ring finger, 5—little finger.

MUSICAL METER

As you sing "Du, Du, Liegst Mir im Herzen" and clap the rhythm of the beat you will feel the beats falling into accent groupings which you can count as "ONE-Two-Three," "ONE-Two-Three," the first beat being accented and the second and third unaccented.

Du,	Du,	liegst mir im	Herz - en
>	>	>	>
1 2 3	1 2 3	1 2 3	1 2 3

The way you conduct three-beat rhythm is: "DOWN-Right-Up."

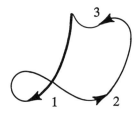

The down-beat, ONE, is heavy and the other beats are light. Practice this conducting pattern as you sing the song again.

"How Does My Lady's Garden Grow?" is another song in which the beat-rhythm falls into accent groupings of threes.

HOW DOES MY LADY'S GARDEN GROW?

This melody may not be familiar to you and you may have to learn it "by ear," i.e., with the assistance of someone who can read music and can sing or play it for you until you have the melody memorized. Failing this, you might be able to learn it by yourself with the help of the bells or the piano. All the tones in this song belong to the scale of C which you already know. Review what you learned about this and the names for the various scale degrees (see p. 10). The letter names might be particularly helpful because they are easy to associate with both the notation and the instrument. Try this.

Next, scan the words of the song and note how the word-rhythm (melody-rhythm) and beat-rhythm are related:

How does my	la - dy's	gar - den	grow?
>	>	>	>
1 2 3	1 2 3	1 2 3	1 2 3

After you have learned the song in one of these ways, practice singing it with the three-beat conducting pattern.

By now you have learned that the rhythm of the beat falls into regularly recurring groups of accented and unaccented beats. These repeated groups of beats, or accent groupings, constitute the *meter* in music. When a melody moves in groups of two beats, it is in *duple meter;* when it moves in three beats, it is *triple meter.* Other groupings of beats are possible as we shall discover further on.

RHYTHMIC NOTATION

As you sang and played the songs in this and the preceding chapter, you may have observed that the notation of the melodies contained other symbols for duration than those discussed in connection with "Go Tell Aunt Rhody." (See p. 4.) All such symbols are related and belong to our system of rhythmic notation which includes *notes, rests,* and *meter signatures.* Familiarity with these symbols is essential for interpreting the musical score.

Duration of Notes and Rests. Rhythm can be defined as a sequence of sounds (tones) and silences (rests) of varying duration controlled by an underlying beat or pulsation. The duration (*time values*) of these sounds and silences are symbolized in notation by notes and rests of various shapes:

whole note	half note	quarter note	eighth note	sixteenth note	thirty-second note

whole rest	half rest	quarter rest	eighth rest	sixteenth rest	thirty-second rest

These symbols do not represent exact durations of sounds and silences; they only indicate relationships. The *relative duration* of the notes (note or time values) may be seen from this:

1 whole note

equals

2 half notes

or

4 quarter notes

or

8 eighth notes

or

16 sixteenth notes

The relative duration of the equivalent rest values would be the same.

Ties and Dots. Tones may be prolonged by connecting two notes of the same pitch with a curved line called a *tie:* [2]

The second note is not sounded separately; the first pitch is merely sustained for the total value of the two notes.

A *dot* after a note or a rest increases its value one half:

$$\text{𝅗𝅥.} = \text{𝅗𝅥} + \text{♩}\qquad \text{𝄼.} = \text{𝄼} + \text{𝄽}$$

$$\text{♩.} = \text{♩} + \text{♪}\qquad \text{𝄽.} = \text{𝄽} + \text{𝄾}$$

$$\text{♪.} = \text{♪} + \text{♬}\qquad \text{𝄾.} = \text{𝄾} + \text{𝄿}$$

$$\text{♬.} = \text{♬} + \text{𝅘𝅥𝅲}\qquad \text{𝄿.} = \text{𝄿} + \text{𝅀}$$

[2] When two notes of different pitches are connected, both are sounded and these notes are said to be *slurred:*

Meter or Time Signature. In music notation, the rhythmic flow of tones and rests is measured off into equal time intervals by vertical lines drawn through the staff. These are called *bar lines,* and the note and rest values contained between two such lines make up a *measure.* A *double bar* is used to denote the ending of a song or an instrumental composition or the ending of a section of a lengthy musical work.[3]

At the beginning of the notation of a song or instrumental composition there are two numbers, one above the other, which are referred to as the *meter signature* or *time signature.* The lower number of this signature represents a note value, usually one that represents the *beat unit,* and the upper number indicates the number of such notes, or their equivalents, which are to be found in each measure. In the above illustration the meter signature is $\frac{3}{4}$. This tells us that the beat unit is a quarter note (♩) and that each measure will contain three such notes, or their equivalents. In other words, each measure is made up of three quarter note beats (♩♩♩). A three-beat measure is an example of triple meter which is made up of accent groupings of "ONE-Two-Three." Note that this gives added meaning to the function of the bar lines: it divides the music into metric units of accented and unaccented beats. The beat following the bar line is accented and the beat preceding the bar line is unaccented.

The songs which we have sung and played thus far have exemplified the use of these meter signatures: $\frac{2}{4}$, $\frac{3}{4}$, and $\frac{3}{8}$. Examine the songs again and note the function of the signatures.

$\frac{2}{4}$ indicates two beats to the measure and that a quarter note (♩) will receive one beat ($\frac{2}{♩}$).

[3] Two types of double bars are used: between sections within a composition two light lines are used (‖); at the end of the composition one light and one heavy line is used (‖).

26

Example: "Deaf Woman's Courtship"

$\frac{3}{4}$ indicates three beats to the measure and that a quarter note (𝅘𝅥) will receive one beat ($\frac{3}{\text{𝅘𝅥}}$).

Example: "Du, Du, Liegst mir im Herzen"

$\frac{3}{8}$ indicates three beats to the measure and that an eighth note (𝅘𝅥𝅮) will receive one beat ($\frac{3}{\text{𝅘𝅥𝅮}}$).

Example: "How Does My Lady's Garden Grow?"

THE UP-BEAT OR ANACRUSIS

All the previous songs have started on the first beat of the measure. However, many of the songs that you will use in the classroom start on other parts of the measure, usually on the last beat, or on a fraction of the last beat. Such songs are said to begin with an *up-beat* or *anacrusis*. "Billy Boy" begins on the last beat of the measure. Note that the last measure contains only one beat. The reason for this is that when a song begins on an incomplete measure, the last measure will complete this measure.

BILLY BOY

English Folk Song

Oh___ where have you been, Bil - ly Boy, Bil - ly Boy,

Oh___ where have you been, charm - ing Bil - ly?___

I have been to seek a wife, She's the joy___ of my life,

She's a young thing and can - not leave her moth - er.___

2. Did she bid you to come in,
   Billy Boy, Billy Boy?
   Yes, she bid me to come in;
   There's a dimple in her chin:

3. Can she make a cherry pie,
   Billy Boy, Billy Boy?
   She can make a cherry pie,
   quick as cat can wink her eye:

4. Can she cook and can she spin,
   Billy Boy, Billy Boy?
   She can cook and she can spin,
   she can do most anything:

5. How old is she,
   Billy Boy, Billy Boy?
   Three time six and four times seven,
   twenty-eight and eleven:

28

"Good-Bye, Ol' Paint," which also begins on the last beat of a three-beat measure, has a verse and a refrain. Note that the half note in the last measure of the refrain completes the incomplete first measure.

GOOD-BYE, OL' PAINT

Smoothly

Cowboy Song

My foot in the stir - rup, my po - ny won't stan';___

I'm a - leav - in' Chey - enne an' I'm off for Mon - tan'.___

Good - bye, ol' Paint, I'm a - leav - ing' Chey - enne.

2. I'm riding ol' Paint and a-leading ol' Fan;
   Goodbye, little Annie, I'm off to Montan'.

3. Go hitch up your horses and give them some hay,
   And seat yourself by me as long as you stay.

Observe the double bars with dots at the beginning and end of the refrain. These are *repeat signs* and they indicate that the passage between the two signs should be repeated. If a song or section of a composition is to be repeated from the beginning, only one sign is necessary, the one with dots at the left of the double bar.

When conducting songs which begin with an incomplete measure, the preparatory beat should be given in the direction of the preceding "imaginary" beat.

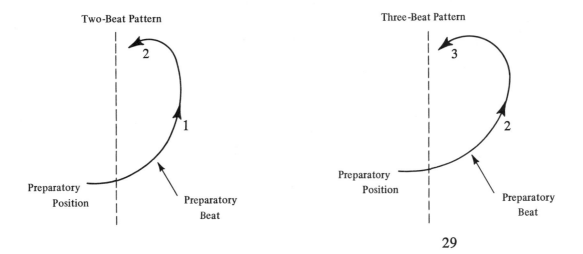

Two-Beat Pattern

Three-Beat Pattern

Preparatory Position

Preparatory Beat

Preparatory Position

Preparatory Beat

Another common meter signature is $\frac{4}{4}$, which indicates that there is to be four beats in the measure and that a quarter note will receive one beat ($\frac{4}{\text{♩}}$). A melody which moves in fours is said to be in *quadruple meter*. "A Cradle Hymn" is an example of such a melody.

A CRADLE HYMN

Slowly   J. S. Bach

Hush, my dear, lie still and slum-ber, Ho-ly an-gels__ guard thy bed.

Heav'n-ly bless-ings with-out num-ber gen-tly fall-ing__ on thy__head.

2. How much better thou'rt attended
   Than the Son of God could be,
   When from heaven He descended
   And became a child like thee.

3. Mayest thou like to know and fear Him,
   Trust and love Him all thy days,
   Then go dwell forever near Him
   See His face and sing His praise.

Words by Isaac Watts

As you sing this song you will sense that both the first and third beats are accented, although there seems to be less "stress" on the third beat than on the first. We say there is a *primary accent* on the first beat and a *secondary accent* on the third beat. The second and fourth beats will be felt to be unaccented. The over-all feeling of the beat-rhythm is an accent grouping which may be counted as "ONE-Two-*Three*-Four."

$$\begin{array}{c|cccc|cccc|}
 & \text{Hush,} & \text{my} & \text{dear,} & \text{lie} & \text{still} & \text{and} & \text{slum-} & \text{ber} \\
\frac{4}{4} & > & & \wedge & & > & & \wedge & \\
 & 1 & 2 & 3 & 4 & 1 & 2 & 3 & 4
\end{array}$$

You conduct four beats in the following manner: "DOWN-Left-*Right*-Up."

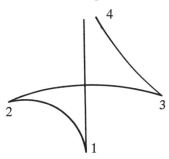

"White Coral Bells" also moves in fours. Practice the four-beat conducting pattern by leading two groups of singers in this favorite two-part round.

WHITE CORAL BELLS

Andante [4]

Two-Part Round

1. White cor - al bells up - on a slen - der stalk,
2. Oh, don't you wish that you could hear them ring?

Lil - ies of the val - ley deck my gar - den walk,
That will hap - pen on - ly when the fair - ies sing.

Sometimes a $\frac{4}{4}$ meter signature may be represented by a symbol which has the appearance of a capital "C." This symbol (**C**) is interchangeable with $\frac{4}{4}$ (see p. 40).

Simple Meters. The meters discussed so far, duple, triple, and quadruple, are called *simple meters* in contradistinction to *compound meters* which we shall consider next. But before concluding our discussion of simple meters we must call attention to another meter signature which is often used to represent duple meter. This is the $\frac{2}{2}$ signature which indicates that there should be two beats in the measure and that a half note ( ) will receive one beat ($\frac{2}{2}$). Sometimes the symbol (**¢**) will be used to represent $\frac{2}{2}$ meter, in which case it is called *alla breve*.

The conductor's beat for $\frac{2}{2}$ is the same as for $\frac{2}{4}$.

---

[4] *Andante* means moderately slow. See Appendix B.

31

JINGLE AT THE WINDOWS

Moderato

Singing Game

Pass one win - dow, ti - de - o, Pass two win - dows, ti - de - o,

Pass three win - dows, ti - de - o, Jin - gle at the win - dows, ti - de - o.

Ti - de - o, ti - de - o, Jin - gle at the win - dows, ti - de - o,

Ti - de - o, ti - de - o, Jin - gle at the win - dows, ti - de - o.

SHORT'NIN' BREAD

Plantation Song

Two lit - tle chil - dren just a - ly - in' in bed,
One lit - tle fel - low just a - ly - in' in bed,

One of them sick an' the oth - er mos' dead.
When he hear tell of the short' - nin' bread,

Call for the doc - tor an' the doc - tor said,
Pop up so live - ly an' he dance an' sing,

32

"Feed them chil - dren on short' - nin bread."
Al - mos' cut him the pig - eon wing.

REFRAIN

Mam - my's lit - tle ba - by loves short' - nin', short' - nin',

Mam - my's lit - tle ba - by loves short - nin', bread.

Compound Meters. The meter signature does not always indicate the proper number of beats to be found in a measure. For example, the meter signature for "Row, Row, Row Your Boat" is $\frac{6}{8}$ which indicates that there should be six beats in each measure and that an eighth note (♪) should receive one beat ($\frac{6}{8}$).

Row,_____ row,_____ row____ your boat,_____
1   2   3   4   5   6   1   2   3   4   5   6

But, when you sing this familiar round, you do not ordinarily feel six beats to the measure, only two. In other words, the dotted quarter note (♩.) becomes the beat unit rather than the eighth note, and this gives you a feeling of duple meter:

Row,_____ row,_____ row____ your boat,_____
1   2   1   2

However, as you sing the last phrase you can feel an underlying pulsation of "three" within the dotted quarter note beat unit.

Mer - ri - ly, mer - ri - ly, mer - ri - ly, mer - ri - ly
(1   2   3) (4   5   6) (1   2   3) (4   5   6)
1   2   1   2

33

Try singing "Row, Row, Row Your Boat" as you clap the beat, first with six beats to the measure and then with two. You will probably sense that the latter is more appropriate to the rhythmic flow of the melody.

ROW, ROW, ROW YOUR BOAT

Four-Part Round

Row, Row, row your boat Gent - ly down the stream.___

Mer- ri - ly, mer- ri - ly, mer- ri - ly, mer- ri - ly, Life is but a dream.___

Thus $\frac{6}{8}$ meter is in reality two meters of three pulsations combined to form a meter of six pulsations. For this reason, $\frac{6}{8}$ meter gives the impression of having two accented beats. The first beat is marked by a strong, *primary accent,* while the fourth beat has a weaker, *secondary accent.*

A combination of two simple (triple) meters such as this is called *compound duple meter,* i.e. a meter with two beats, each divided into three equal pulsations. Other compound meters are $\frac{9}{8}$, called *compound triple meter*

and $\frac{12}{8}$ meter, called *compound quadruple meter*

but these are used only infrequently in the song literature for elementary schools.[5]

[5] For songs in $\frac{9}{8}$ meter, see "Down in the Valley" (p. 76) and "The Canadian" (p. 181).

A summary chart of the various meters may be found at the end of this chapter. Study this chart with the following in mind:

1. A simple meter is one in which the upper number of the meter signature is 2, 3, or 4.

2. A compound meter is one in which the upper number of the meter signature is 6, 9, or 12.

Our next song, "Rosa, Come and Go Dancing," is also in $\frac{6}{8}$ meter. Although it moves at a more leisurely pace than "Row, Row, Row Your Boat," it still gives a feeling of moving in twos rather than in sixes.

ROSA, COME AND GO DANCING

Flemish Folk Song

"Ros - a, come and go danc - ing, go danc - ing, go danc - ing,

Ros - a, come and go danc - ing, Please dance with me!"

Ros - a shook her pret - ty head, "I'm choos - ing my part - ner,

sir," she said. "It might be you!"

The conducting pattern most often used for $\frac{6}{8}$ meter is the same as that used for $\frac{2}{4}$ meter, "DOWN-Up," with the heavier down-beat on the primary accent and the lighter up-beat on the secondary accent. However, some songs move at such a slow pace that they require a different conducting pattern, one in which each of the six pulses (eighth notes) within the $\frac{6}{8}$ meter is

6 *D.C. al Fine*, from the beginning to *Fine*, the end. See Appendix B.

felt. Our next song, "Cradle Song," is such a song. The six-beat pattern is conducted in this way: DOWN-Left-Left-*Right*-Right-Up.

CRADLE SONG

DIVISIONS OF THE BEAT UNIT

The various beat units ($\downarrow$, $\downarrow\cdot$, $\downarrow$, $\downarrow$) may be divided in many different ways to create interesting rhythmic patterns.

Equal Divisions. In the songs you have had thus far, the quarter and half note beats have usually been divided equally into twos and fours, and the dotted quarter note was divided into threes:

Love Somebody

Occasionally there will be *three* notes of equal value within a beat unit which is normally divided into twos:

Such notes are called *triplets* and are designated by a number "3" over the notes which are contained within the beat. Therefore, a group of three notes to be played or sung in the place of two of the *same kind* is a called a triplet.

"Sing, Sing Together" is an example of a melody containing triplets.

SING, SING TOGETHER

English Round

Sing, sing to - geth - er, Mer - ri - ly, mer - ri - ly sing;

Sing, sing to - geth - er, Mer - ri - ly, mer - ri - ly sing;

Sing, sing, sing, sing!

Unequal Divisions. Unequal divisions of the beat unit are also very common. The four sixteenth notes within the quarter note beat may be joined in the following ways to create new rhythmic patterns:

Some of these new rhythmic patterns occur in "Grandma Grunts." Study the notation closely to discover on which beats these occur; then clap the melody-rhythm several times through as you count the beat.

GRANDMA GRUNTS

Spirited

North Carolina Mountain Song

Grand-ma Grunts said a cur-i-ous thing,"Boys can whis-tle but girls must sing."

That is what I heard her say, "Twas no long-er than yes-ter-day.

REFRAIN

Boys can whis-tle (whistle) Girls must sing, tra la la la la!

2. Boys can whistle, of course they may,
They can whistle the livelong day.
Why can't girls whistle too, pray tell,
If they manage to do it well?

3. Grandma Grunts said it wouldn't do,
Gave a very good reason too:
Whistling girls and crowing hens
Always come to some bad ends.

The three eighth notes within the dotted quarter note beat may be joined in two ways:

The first pattern figures prominently in most songs in $\frac{6}{8}$ meter (see "Rosa, Come and Go Dancing"), but the second pattern occurs less frequently, and when it does it gives a syncopated (see below) effect to the rhythm as in the fifth measure of "Hunting Song."

HUNTING SONG

Three-Part Round

With a bounce

Mer-ri-ly, mer-ri-ly greet the morn, Cheer-i-ly, cheer-i-ly sound the horn.

Hark! to the ech-oes, hear them play, O'er hill and dale and far a-way.

SYNCOPATION

Syncopation is the result of displaced accents within the measure. Accents may be shifted in the following ways:

1. by accenting a normally weak beat.

2. by having a rest on a strong beat.

3. by holding a weak beat over a strong beat.

4. by tying a weak portion of a beat to a stronger one.

Several interesting rhythmic patterns, not all syncopated, occur in "Hey Lidee." Observe first that the refrain of this song begins on the second beat of a four-beat measure and that the first three notes are in an even rhythm. This is followed by a measure of uneven rhythms, the second half measure syncopated. The third measure has the same rhythm as the first, but the fourth measure differs from the second in that the syncopation is advanced one beat. Another syncopated pattern occurs in the second measure of the verse. Study these patterns very carefully; then chant the words rhythmically while clapping the beat. Stomp your foot on the quarter rests.

HEY LIDEE

American Folk Song

2. First you sing a simple line,
   Hey Lidee, Lidee - lo.
   Then you try to make it rhyme
   Hey Lidee, Lidee - lo.

"He's Got the Whole World in His Hands" is characterized by a number of interesting syncopation patterns. Study these by clapping the beat and reciting the words first; then clap the melody-rhythm as you count the beat. Note that this song begins on the second half of the third beat.

HE'S GOT THE WHOLE WORLD IN HIS HANDS

He's got the whole___ world ___ in his hands,___ He's got the

whole__ world___ in his hands,__He's got the whole__ world__

in his hands, __ He's got the whole world in his hands. __

2. He's got the wind and rain in his hands.

3. He's got both you and me in his hands.

41

The refrain of "Li'l 'Liza Jane" contains two similar, yet somewhat different syncopated patterns:

In the first pattern there is a quarter rest on the first beat which must be observed carefully in order to achieve the syncopated effect on "Oh!" As you sing the song, clap your hands or stomp your feet on this rest to avoid a premature entry on the refrain.

LI'L 'LIZA JANE

2. I got a house in Baltimore, Li'l 'Liza Jane,
   Brussels carpet on my floor, Li'l 'Liza Jane.

3. I got a house in Baltimore, Li'l 'Liza Jane,
   Silver doorplate on my door, Li'l 'Liza Jane.

4. Come, my love, and marry me, Li'l 'Liza Jane,
   And I'll take good care of thee, Li'l 'Liza Jane.

By now you have explored most of the metric-rhythm patterns that you are likely to encounter. The following chart may help to summarize what we have learned about musical meter and rhythm in this chapter and also serve as a reference for future use.

DUPLE METER

TRIPLE METER

QUADRUPLE METER

DEVELOPING SKILLS

SINGING

1. Sing the songs with appropriate expressiveness paying particular attention to rhythmic accuracy, tempo, and phrasing.

2. Practice the conducting patterns for the various meters as you sing the songs.

3. Sing the melodies with number and syllable names.

4. Practice singing and conducting the rounds learned so far with special attention to bringing in the various parts.

PLAYING

1. Practice playing the melodies on bells and piano.

2. Practice playing accompaniments on the Autoharp and piano while you or others sing the songs.

3. Practice playing some of the songs with melody and chords together.

4. Add suitable percussion instruments as an accompaniment to singing and playing songs.

READING

1. Insert bar lines to conform with the meter signatures in the following:

2. Establish a steady beat by counting or tapping the foot and clap the following rhythm patterns. After you have mastered each pattern, clap all the patterns in the same meters in succession without stopping between them.

3. After establishing an appropriate beat, count and clap (or play) the following four measure rhythm phrases. Also practice performing them as duets by two individuals or groups, one taking the top line, the other the bottom line. Perform these duets with percussion instruments as well, using a different instrument for each part.

WRITING

1. Complete the following measures with appropriate notes:

2. Complete the following measures with appropriate rests:

3. Transcribe the notation for "Row, Row, Row Your Boat" to the bass clef.

VOCABULARY

Define or explain the following musical terms:

anacrusis	meter	slur
bar line	meter signature	syncopation
compound meter	quadruple meter	tie
dot (after note)	preparatory beat	triple meter
duple meter	repeat sign	triplet

ANALYTIC-CREATIVE ACTIVITIES

1. Compare the melody-rhythms of the songs in Chapter 1 by clapping any two of them at the same time.

2. Make up as many rhythmic patterns as you can think of in $\frac{2}{4}, \frac{3}{4}, \frac{4}{4}$, and $\frac{6}{8}$ meters.

3. Explore the rhythm of words: names of people, animals, geographical locations, foods, and other subject categories. Notate the rhythm patterns in appropriate meters. Experiment with these, singly and in combinations, in speech and with percussion instruments.

Example:

Moz - art, Hay - dn,   Gluck and Bach;   Schu - mann, Liszt, Rach - ma - ni - noff

Schu - bert, Strauss and   Of - fen - bach   Brahms and Rim - sky   Kor - sa - koff.

4. There are three rhythms in every song: the rhythm of the first beat of the measure, the rhythm of the meter, and the rhythm of the melody. Orchestrate these different rhythms of selected songs from Chapters 1 and 2 for percussion instruments.

Example:

DEAF WOMAN'S COURTSHIP

3

Intervals, Scales, and Chords

A scale can sometimes take the shape of a melody or part of a melody. Sing "The Swan" in unison and observe that it contains all the tones of the C major scale: C, D, E, F, G, A, B, C.

THE SWAN

Sweet-ly the swan sings, Do-de-ah-do, do-de-ah-do, do-de-ah-do.

INTERVALS AND THE MAJOR SCALE

As you sang you probably noticed the wide upward leap between the last note in the first measure and the first note in the second measure: C to C. While both tones are named C, they obviously represent two different pitches, the second one being higher than the first. The pitch distance between two notes or tones is called an *interval*. Intervals are named according to the number of staff degrees which they encompass. If we count the lines and spaces between the low C and the high C (including both these notes), we find that this interval encompasses eight staff degrees. Such an interval is called an *octave*.

The repeated C's in the first measure of "The Swan" are called *unisons*.

Sing the song again and notice how the melody progresses in a descending step-wise fashion on "Do-de-ah-do." The intervals between each syllable are called *seconds* because they encompass only two staff degrees: C to B, B to A, and A to G. Examine the next two "do-de-ah-do" measures and observe that they are exact repetitions of the first one, only beginning on a lower tone. Such repetitions of a group of tones or motives are called *sequences*. Each of these motives encompasses an interval of a *fourth:* C to G, A to E, and F to C.

In the context of the melody these fourths would be referred to as *descending* intervals, while the previous octave was an *ascending* interval.

Intervals similarly numbered may differ in the way they sound. For example, all seconds do not sound alike, a fact that is easily verified at the piano keyboard. Let us compare the intervals E to F and A to B, both seconds:

We see that there is a black key between A and B, while there is no key between E and F. Now, the distance from one key to its nearest neighbor, whether black or white key, is called a *half step* (minor second). Therefore, the distance between E and F is a half step whereas the distance between A and B is two half steps or a *whole step* (major second). Play these two intervals on the piano or bells and listen to the difference in quality between these two seconds.

The Major Scale Pattern. As you look at the piano keyboard you will notice that the notes for the C major scale coincide with the eight white keys from C to C:

Examination of these keys reveals that the distance between them is as follows:

1		2		3		4		5		6		7		8
	whole step		whole step		half step		whole step		whole step		whole step		half step	

This arrangement of tones in a scale is known as the *major scale pattern* and all major scales must conform to this. Other scales are constructed on different patterns, as we shall see further on.

Active and Passive Scale Tones. Sing the ascending major scale and stop momentarily on *ti* (7).

As you sustain this tone you will notice that it has a strong tendency to want to move up to *do* (8) which, when sung, gives the impression of finality or repose to the ascending scale. *Do,* the tonic, is sometimes referred to as the "home-tone"; *ti,* the seventh degree, being only a half step away from the tonic has acquired a special name: *leading tone,* so called due to its strong tendency to move toward the home-tone.

Individual scale tones have different characteristics: some, like *ti,* are *active* (moving) tones; others, like *do,* are *passive* (restful) tones. The active scale tones are *re* (2), *fa* (4), *la* (6), and *ti* (7). The passive scale tones are *do* (1, 8), *mi* (3), and *so* (5). A feeling for individual tendencies of scale tones is a valuable aid to music reading.

Sing the following tonal groups quite slowly and sustain the tone under the fermata until you can "feel" what to sing next (up or down) in order to provide a satisfactory *resolution* for the *suspension* created by the prolonged tone.

As you sang these tonal groups you sensed that *re* (2) tends to move up to *mi* (3) or down to *do* (1); that *fa* (4) has a tendency to move down to *mi* (3) or up to *so* (5); and that *la* (6) seems to want to move down to *so* (5) or up to *ti* (7), which, in turn, would move up to *do* (8).

In summary: active scale tones have a tendency to move to the nearest passive tone. Becoming sensitive to this natural movement or tendency of scale tones is one of the many factors involved in developing note-reading skill.[1]

[1] In certain European countries *hand signals* are used to denote the degrees of the major scale. These hand signals may be found in Appendix A.

Now apply what you have learned about active and passive scale tones to the reading of "Alphabet Song" and "Come Follow Me."

ALPHABET SONG

Allegretto

Mozart

A B C D E F G H I J

K L M N O K L M N O P Q K L M N

O P Q R S T U V W___ X__ Y__ and__ Z

COME, FOLLOW ME

Gaily

John Hilton

Come, fol - low, fol - low, fol - low, Fol - low, fol - low, fol - low me!

Whith - er shall I fol - low, fol - low, fol - low, Whith - er shall I fol - low, fol - low thee?

To the green - wood, to the green - wood, To the green - wood, green - wood tree.

The black keys on the piano also play a role in interval and scale construction. They derive their names from their adjacent white keys by the addition of *accidentals*. These are the *sharp* (♯) which raises the pitch of a note one half step and the *flat* (♭) which lowers the pitch of a note one half step. A sharp placed before F indicates that the next key to the right (a half step higher) should be played, and a flat placed before G indicates that the next key to the left (a half step lower) should be played. Thus, the black key situated between F and G may be referred to by two different names: F-sharp *or* G-flat. Similarly, all black keys have two names. The white keys B, F, and E may also be named in relation to their immediate neighbors one half step above or below by the use of accidentals. The following illustration shows how accidentals appear on the staff and where notes with sharps and flats may be found on the keyboard.

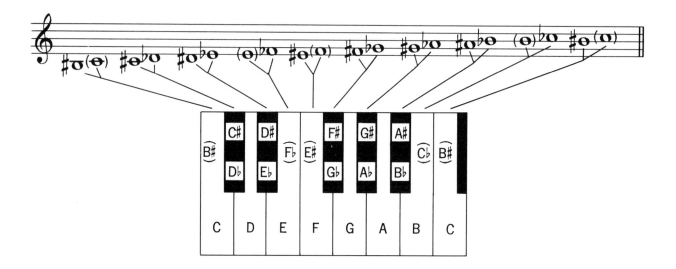

Observe that on the staff the accidental is placed *in front* of the note which is to be altered, whereas in naming the note in question the accidental is mentioned *after* the note name.

Accidentals are sometimes referred to as *chromatic alterations*. They also include the following symbols: the *natural* (♮) which is used to cancel the effect of either a sharp or flat; the *double sharp* (✕) which raises a note a whole step; and the *double flat* (♭♭) which lowers a note one whole step.

The C major scale is made up of whole and half steps and does not require any accidentals. Such a scale is called a *diatonic scale*. A scale which is made up entirely of half steps is called a *chromatic scale*. Chromatic scales may be notated in two different ways: with sharps or with flats. Sharps are usually used for the ascending scale and flats for the descending scale. You are already familiar with the syllables applied to the major scale. When accidentals appear in the notation, the syllables are altered as follows:

From this you can see that whenever a sharp occurs the vowel changes to *i* (pronounced as *ee*) and that when a flat is used the vowel changes to *e* (pronounced as in *day*) except for the syllable *re* which changes to *rah*. Sing this chromatic scale ascending and descending several times so that you are quite sure of the syllable alterations.

THE WHOLE-TONE SCALE

The whole-tone scale is a six-note scale, each step being one whole tone from the other. Compositions based on this scale reveal lack of any definite tonal center. The impressionist composers, Debussy, Ravel, Delius, and others, liked to use it in their compositions (see Chapter 13).

WHOLE-TONE SCALE

TYPES OF INTERVALS

Let us now consider various types of intervals that you should be familiar with.

Major-Scale Intervals. Intervals have general names which are determined by counting the lines and spaces including the two notes which form the interval. Examples:

But, as we already have observed in the case of seconds, intervals of the same name may have different *qualities* (sounds) because they contain a different number of half steps. To describe these different qualities of intervals five terms are used: *Perfect, Major, Minor, Augmented,* and *Diminished.* After determining the general name of the interval by counting the lines and spaces, we can determine its quality as follows:

1. Consider the lowest note of the interval as *do* or 1 of a major scale.

2. When the upper note occurs in this scale, seconds, thirds, sixths, and sevenths are called *major* intervals; unisons (primes), fourths, fifths, and octaves are called *perfect* intervals.

Perfect Prime   Major 2nd   Major 3rd   Perfect 4th   Perfect 5th   Major 6th   Major 7th   Perfect Octave

3. Major intervals lowered one half step become *minor,* and perfect intervals lowered one half step become *diminished.*

Minor 2nd   Minor 3rd   Diminished 4th   Diminished 5th   Minor 6th   Minor 7th   Diminished Octave

4. Major and perfect intervals raised one half step become *augmented.*

Aug. Prime   Aug. 2nd   Aug. 3rd   Aug. 4th   Aug. 5th   Aug. 6th   Aug. 7th   Aug. Octave

A knowledge of the basic intervals and the ability to recognize and hear them are very helpful in learning to read music and in part-singing. To help you remember the sound of some of the more important intervals, learn to associate them with specific songs that you know. The minor third may be found in:

Lul - la - by   and   good   night

56

LIGHTLY ROW

Light - ly row, light - ly row,

The major third and minor third in:

CHILDREN'S PRAYER

When at night I go to sleep

The perfect fourth is very common as the starting interval in songs such as:

AULD LANG SYNE

Should auld ac-quain-tance be for-got

THE FARMER IN THE DELL

The farm - er in the dell

The perfect fifth is very familiar to anyone who has heard a violinist tune up:

TWINKLE, TWINKLE LITTLE STAR

Twink - le twink - le lit - tle star

FOR UNTO US A CHILD IS BORN

For un - to us a Child is born___

The major sixth is quite common as a beginning interval:

MY BONNIE

My Bon - nie lies   o - ver the   o - cean

THE OLD OAKEN BUCKET

How   dear   to   my   heart

Melodic and Harmonic Intervals. When the two tones of an interval are sounded one after the other, it is called a *melodic interval;* when the two tones are sounded together, it is called a *harmonic interval.* The two notes of harmonic intervals are usually written one above the other; however, primes and seconds are written with the notes placed next to each other.

Inversion of Intervals. The position of the tones of a harmonic interval may be exchanged. The bottom note may be moved up an octave or the top note may be moved down an octave. Such an exchange of positions is called an *inversion* and the interval is said to be *inverted.* The interval is inverted *upward* when the bottom note is placed an octave higher and it is inverted *downward* when the top note is placed an octave lower.

From this we can see that when intervals are inverted, perfect intervals remain perfect, major intervals become minor, and minor intervals become major.

Melodies are often harmonized by using parallel thirds and sixths. Here are two examples of songs arranged in this manner for two-part singing. The melody is in the upper part in both songs.

SAN SERENI

San Se - re - ni, de la bue - na, bue - na vi - da,

Ha - cen a - si, a - si los za - pa - te - ros. A -

si, a - si, a - si, a - si me gus - ta a - mi.

AU CLAIR DE LA LUNE

Au clair de la lu - ne, Mon a - mi Pier - rot,

Prê - te - moi ta plu - me Pour é - crire un mot.

Ma chan - delle est mor - te, Je n'ai plus de feu;

Ou - vre - moi ta por - te Pour l'a - mour de Dieu.

Intervals play an important role in the building of chords. Chords may be made up of any number of tones in many different arrangements, but we shall concern ourselves here with only two kinds of chords, *triads* and *seventh chords*. You have been using both kinds of chords, the C and the G₇ chords, for accompaniments to the songs in the previous chapters, but without detailed knowledge or explanation of their construction. Let us now see how they are made up.

Triads. A triad is a three-tone chord and the familiar C chord is an example of a triad. When we examine this chord in detail, we discover that it is made up of two harmonic intervals sounded simultaneously:

As you can see, this triad can be described in two ways.[2] The preferred definition is that it is made up of a major third and a perfect fifth; or it may be said to consist of a major third and a minor third. The separate tones of the triad are designated as *root* (lowest tone), *third* (middle tone), and *fifth* (top tone).

Types of Triads. Triads may be built on any tone of a scale and are designated by letter names or Roman numerals according to their roots:

Notice that on the staff a triad involves three consecutive lines or spaces: *line-line-line* or *space-space-space*. This is an important visual concept to keep in mind when learning to read music.

Play these triads on the piano and listen to the quality or sound of each. The I, IV, and V chords have the same kind of sound because they are all composed of the same type of intervals: a major third and a perfect fifth. Check this on the keyboard.

[2] Remember that in analyzing intervals and triads we always begin with the lowest note and figure *up* from this note.

60

A triad composed of a major third and a perfect fifth is called a *major triad*.

The II, III, and VI chords also have the same quality but are different from that of the major triads because these triads contain a *minor* third and a perfect fifth.

A triad composed of a minor third and a perfect fifth is called a *minor triad*.

The VII chord is neither major nor minor. It is composed of a minor third and a diminished fifth and is therefore called a *diminished triad*.

To summarize: a major triad is composed of a major third and a perfect fifth; a minor triad is composed of a minor third and a perfect fifth; and a diminished triad is composed of a minor third and a diminished fifth. It is also worth remembering that a major triad becomes a minor triad when its third is lowered one half step; a minor triad becomes a major triad when its third is raised one half step; and a minor triad becomes a diminished triad when its fifth is lowered one half step.

Seventh Chords. The G_7 chord you have been using for your accompaniments is a four-note chord and therefore is not a triad, but a *seventh chord*. Seventh chords may be built on any note of the scale and the various chords, as with the triads, would have different qualities. However, a detailed discussion of these would have little practical value. On the other hand, the seventh chord built on the fifth degree of the scale, the V_7 chord (or *dominant seventh chord*), is used so frequently in song accompaniments that you should be very familiar with its construction.

The G_7 chord is built on the fifth degree of the C major scale; therefore it is the V_7 chord in this key. Let us see how it is constructed:

As you can see it is made up of a major third, a perfect fifth, and a minor seventh. Another way of describing it is to say that it consists of a major triad with a minor third added.

The four tones of a seventh chord are designated *root, third, fifth,* and *seventh* and the chord is named a seventh chord because of the interval of a seventh added above the root.

Chord Inversions. All the chords we have discussed so far have been presented in root position, i.e. with the root at the bottom of the chord. However, the tones of a chord may be arranged in different ways without destroying its quality or aural identity.

A triad may assume three positions: *root, first inversion,* and *second inversion.* You are already familiar with the root positions of triads. When the third of the triad appears as the lowest note, the chord is in its first inversion; when the fifth appears as the lowest tone, the chord is in its second inversion.

Another way to identify chord positions is to observe the placement of the chord root:

Root at the bottom—root position

Root on top—first inversion

Root in the middle—second inversion

Explore these positions of a triad at the keyboard.

A seventh chord may assume four positions: *root, first inversion, second inversion,* and *third inversion.* As in the case of a triad, a seventh chord is in its first inversion when the third appears as the lowest tone and in its second inversion when the fifth is the lowest tone. When the seventh appears as the lowest tone, it is in its third inversion.

Note that the G_7 (V_7) chord you have been using for the song accompaniments has been the first inversion of this chord with the fifth (D) omitted.

Familiarity with triads and seventh chords, and their inversions, is a great help in learning to read music and in harmonizing melodies. (Harmonizing melodies is discussed in Chapter 10.) In learning to read music we distinguish between "scale-line" melodies (melodies which progress step-wise along a scale) and "chord-line" melodies (melodies which follow the outline of a chord as it progresses). The melodies at the beginning of this chapter (as well as many of the melodies in the first two chapters) were of the scale-line type. But some of the songs you have been singing also represented the chord-line type. Examine again the beginning measures of "Love Somebody" (p. 1), "Grandma Grunts" (p. 38), "Whistle, Daughter, Whistle" (p. 6) and "Deaf Woman's Courtship" (p. 2) and you will see that they move along the tones of the triad on C (I chord).

"Planting Cabbages" is a song with a melody that represents an even mixture of chord-line and scale-line tonal movement. Try to read this song "at sight" without the aid of an instrument.

PLANTING CABBAGES

Gently swaying

French Folk Song

Can you plant the cab-bage so, Just as we do, just as we do?

Can you plant the cab-bage so, Just the same as we can do?

2. You can plant it with your feet. . . .

3. You can plant it with your hands . . .

Here is a well-known melody, "Taps," which is based almost entirely on the second inversion of the C triad.

TAPS

Slowly

U. S. Army Bugle Call

Day is done, gone the sun from the lake from the hills,

from the sky. Safe-ly rest all is well, God is nigh.

Which part of the melody outlines the root position?

DEVELOPING SKILLS

SINGING

1. Sing the melodies with both number names and syllables.

2. Practice singing and conducting the rounds in this chapter with special attention to bringing in the parts at the proper time.

3. Sing the following intervals with number and syllable names as written and with the suggested rhythmic variations.

4. Practice singing the following chromatic sequences with syllables.

PLAYING

1. Play the above intervals and chromatic sequences on the bells and on the piano.

2. Find the C, F, and G triads on the piano (or build them with the Resonator Bells) and play them in root position and in inversions.

3. Play the melodies in this chapter on the bells.

READING

1. Sing the following melodies with syllable, number, and letter names without the aid of an instrument.

(A)   Netherlands

(B)   Germany

(C)   Denmark

(D)   Bohemia

2. Establish an appropriate beat; then clap or play each of the following eight-measure rhythm patterns. When these have been learned, perform them as *rounds,* one group beginning after the first group has sounded two measures. Also perform them as duets.

3. Name the following general intervals.

WRITING

1. Complete writing the general intervals above the given tones.

2. Construct *major* triads on the following tones.

3. Construct *minor* triads on the following tones.

4. Write out the first and second inversions of these major and minor triads.

VOCABULARY

Define or explain the following musical terms:

active tone	interval	sequence
chord root	inversion	seventh chord
chromatic scale	leading tone	sharp (♯)
diatonic scale	major triad	suspension
dominant seventh chord	minor triad	whole step
flat (♭)	passive tone	
half step	resolution	

67

ANALYTIC-CREATIVE ACTIVITIES

1. Play the C major chord on the piano and then find the C *minor* chord by lowering the middle finger one half step. What is the difference between these two chords?

2. Utilize your knowledge of the C minor chord to play the melody of "Go Tell Aunt Rhody" in minor. Why might this be appropriate?

ACTIVITIES FOR TWO INDIVIDUALS OR TWO GROUPS

3. Sing or play "San Sereni" in parallel sixths by adding a second part above the melody at the interval of a sixth.

4. Sing or play "Au Claire de la Lune" in parallel thirds by adding a second part above the melody at the interval of a third.

5. Experiment with singing or playing "Billy Boy" and "Jingle at the Window" in parallel thirds and sixths. What adjustments have to be made in the added parts in order to make them sound "right"?

4

Major Scales and Chording

The songs studied thus far have all been in the key of C major. While this is considered an easy key with which to begin playing such keyboard instruments as bells and piano, most songs are written in other keys in order to place them in more suitable ranges for singing. Songs for children are usually pitched so that the melody can be written between middle C and E in the fourth space of the treble staff, this being the normal range for children's voices.

TRANSPOSING MELODIES

An example of a song written in the key of C that has a range too low for children's voices is "Bow Belinda."

BOW BELINDA

When you sing this song as written, you will no doubt feel that it has been pitched too low for comfort. Let us see what it looks like in number notation:

1 1 3. 5 3 1 2 2 7,. 2 7, 5,

1 1 3. 5 3 1 5 4 3 2 1   1

The range problem occurs in the second measure where the melody goes down to G below middle C (5,). This and the preceding low B (7,) are also out of the range of the more common bell sets. Now, instead of using middle C as the 1 (tonic), let us use the F in the first space of the treble staff as the beginning tone. As you sing the melody with the above numbers in this new key, you will sense that the whole song is higher in pitch and that the low tones you experienced in the key of C have been avoided. Shifting the melody from one key to another by changing the keynote is called *transposition*.

Play the melody on the piano or bells starting on F. Your ear will soon tell you that you must use the black key called B♭ to "make it sound right." To explain why this is necessary we must examine the major scale pattern once again. You will recall that the tones of the major scale were arranged in this manner (see p. 51):

1	2	3	4	5	6	7	8
do	*re*	*mi*	*fa*	*so*	*la*	*ti*	*do*
whole step	whole step	half step	whole step	whole step	whole step	half step	

Let us see what a major scale constructed on F would look like:

In applying the scale-pattern you find that you must play B♭

instead of B because there must be a half step between 3 and 4 (*mi* and *fa*). Confirm this with your ear by playing B and B♭ alternately. This, then, ex-

70

plains why you have to use the black key for 4 when playing "Bow Belinda" in the key of F. The notation of the song in this key looks like this:

BOW BELINDA

Bow,   bow,   bow Be - lin - da;   Bow, bow, bow Be - lin - da.

Bow,   bow,   bow Be - lin - da; Won't you be my part - ner?

Instead of writing in the *flat* (♭) every time it occurs in the melody a *key signature* is used after the clef to indicate that all B's should be "flatted."

The key signature thus tells you which key you are in—in this case you are in the key of F.

If you were to play "Bow Belinda" on the bells or the piano beginning on G, instead of on F, you would have to use another black key, F♯, to make the melody sound right. The reason for this will become apparent if you build a scale on G according to the major scale-pattern:

As you can see, in order to satisfy the requirements of a whole step between 6 (*la*) and 7 (*ti*), and the half step between 7 (*ti*) and 8 (*do*), you must play F♯ instead of F.

Since all F's must be "sharped" in the key of G, this is indicated by the key signature of "one sharp."

Transposed to the key of G, "Bow Belinda" has this notation:

BOW BELINDA

Bow, bow, bow Be - lin - da; Bow, bow, bow Be - lin - da.

Bow, bow, bow Be - lin - da; Won't you be my part - ner?

CHORDING WITH I AND V₇

You are already familiar with the I (tonic) and V₇ (dominant seventh) chords used to accompany the songs written in C major. You will recall that these chords were named according to their roots, the degrees of the scale upon which they were built. Thus, the C chord was called the I chord because it was built on the first degree of the scale of C, and the G₇ chord was referred to as the V₇ chord because it was built on the fifth degree of this scale (see p. 14 and p. 61).

In other keys the I and V_7 chords will have different names because they will be built on other tones. In the key of F major the respective chords would be F and C_7.

In the key of G major the I chord would be G and the V_7 chord would be D_7.

Chording on the Autoharp. To create accompaniments with the Autoharp for "Bow Belinda" transposed to the new keys locate the buttons marked "F" and "C_7" for the key of F and the buttons marked "G" and "D_7" for the key of G. Practice singing and accompanying this song in both keys. The number of strokes used in each measure will depend on the tempo in which you sing the song. Experiment with one, two, or four strokes in each measure. Which suits the spirit of the song best?

With these new keys and chords at your disposal you can enlarge your song repertory significantly. In singing and accompanying the following songs, use this procedure:

1. Establish the beat in an appropriate tempo.

2. Sing the song while conducting the beat.

3. Make up an accompaniment with the proper chords as indicated in the score. Some songs will require a chord on the accented beats only, others may require chords on unaccented beats as well. When a rest occurs on an accented beat, it will require a chord to keep the rhythm of the beat going. An up-beat (anacrusis) does not require a chord (see "Polly Wolly Doodle" and "Down in the Valley").

As you become more accustomed to playing the Autoharp you will realize that every song demands a style of accompaniment appropriate to itself. Quiet and soothing songs demand slow, relaxed strokes; lively and vigorous songs require fast, crisp strokes.

POLLY WOLLY DOODLE

American Folk Song

Oh, I went down South for to see my Sal, sing

Pol - ly wol - ly doo - dle all the day. My Sal - ly am a

spunk - y gal sing Pol - ly wol - ly doo - dle all the

day. Fare thee well, fare thee well, fare thee well my fair - y

fay, For I'm goin' to Lou' - si - an - a, for to

see my Su - sy - an - a, Sing - ing Pol - ly wol - ly doo - dle all the day.

2. Oh, my Sal she is a maiden fair,
Sing Polly-wolly-doodle all the day;
With curling eyes and laughing hair,
Sing Polly-wolly-doodle all the day.

UPWARD TRAIL

Traditional

March tempo

We're on the up-ward trail, We're on the up-ward trail!

Sing-ing, sing-ing, ev-'ry-bo-dy sing-ing, As we go.

Home-ward bound.

SHOO, FLY, DON'T BOTHER ME

American Singing Game

Rhythmically

Shoo, fly, don't both-er me, Shoo, fly, don't both-er me,

Shoo, fly, don't both-er me, for I be-long to some-bo-dy.

I feel, I feel, I feel, I feel like a morn-ing star,

I feel, I feel, I feel, I feel I feel like a morn-ing star. So,

D.C. al Fine[1]

[1] *D.C. al Fine,* from the beginning to *Fine,* the end.

DOWN IN THE VALLEY

Kentucky Folk Song

Down in the val - ley, the val-ley so low, _____ Hang your head

o - ver, hear the wind blow. _____ Hear the wind blow, dear hear the wind

blow, _____ Hang your head o - ver, hear the wind blow. _____

2. Roses love sunshine, violets love dew,
   Angels in heaven know I love you.
   Know I love you, dear, know I love you,
   Angels in heaven know I love you.

3. Build me a castle forty feet high,
   So I may see him as he rides by.
   As he rides by, dear, as he rides by,
   So I may see him as he rides by.

Chording on the Piano. When you were chording with the C and G_7 chords on the piano, the G_7 chord was played in its first inversion in order to make it easy to move from one chord to another. You will recall that the hand stays in the same position for both chords and that changing from one chord to another only involves slight finger movements. Review the *fingerings* for these chords; in notation they are:

How these chords are fingered is of primary importance because, no matter what key we may transpose a song to, *this fingering for the I-V_7-I progression is always the same.*

Now try this fingering formula in the keys of F and G to prove to yourself that the fingering for the I and V₇ chords remains the same for *all* keys.

After practicing these chord changes you will be ready to add piano accompaniments to your singing of all the songs in this chapter up to this point. Some of you will no doubt be able to play both the melody and the chords together.

Here are two songs with easy "five-finger" melodies written out in full piano score. Practice these with both hands in the keys indicated by the key signatures; then transpose them to the two other keys that you now are familiar with.

CRADLE SONG

Rousseau

Gently

Hush my___ babe, lie still and slum - ber,

Ho - ly___ an - gels guard___ thy___ bed.

MERRILY WE ROLL ALONG

CHORDING WITH I AND IV

Sing "Lovely Evening" in unison as expressively as you can, paying particular attention to voice quality and phrasing.

LOVELY EVENING

A new chord is needed to accompany this melody. This is the IV, or B♭ chord, which is built on the fourth degree of F major.

and

The fourth degree of the scale is called the subdominant; thus the IV chord is frequently referred to as the *subdominant chord.*

Chording with I and IV on the Autoharp. Find the buttons marked "F" and "B♭." Place the index finger of your left hand on the first button and the fourth finger on the second button. Practice the chord changes a few times and then make up a suitable accompaniment to "Lovely Evening," letting your ear tell you how many chords you should use in each measure to obtain the most expressive result.

Chording with I and IV at the Piano. To make the change from I to IV and back to I as easily and smoothly as possible at the piano we must re-arrange the tones of the IV chord, i.e. we must use the second inversion of this chord. In the key of F, the I chord (F) and the IV chord (B♭) have the following finger placements for left-hand chording:

In making the change from I to IV the fifth finger (little finger) stays the same, the second finger (index finger) is placed a half step above the third finger, and the first finger (thumb) moves up one whole step.

In the right hand the chords look like this:

Study the fingering to make the change from one chord to the other.

79

Again, it is heartening to know that *these fingerings are applicable in all major keys,* making it relatively easy to transpose songs to other keys. Here is the notation for the I-IV-I chord progression in C major and G major:

After a little practice with these chord changes on the piano, you should have no difficulty making up a satisfactory accompaniment for "Lovely Evening." Some of you will be able to play both the melody and chords together. Using chords alone at first, transpose the song to C major and G major, also.

You will also enjoy singing "Lovely Evening" as a round. Do this without chording at first so that you will be able to listen closely to the blending of the various parts. This is a three-part round in which the second part enters as the first part begins the second phrase (2.) and the third part joins in when the first part reaches the beginning of the third phrase (3.). As you study the melody you will discover that the second phrase is a sequence of the first phrase, i.e. this phrase is repeated one third higher. Sing the two phrases together and note how this sequential construction produces a pleasing progression of thirds:

Next, sing the three phrases together, beginning at the same time, from the notation. The third phrase contains only one melody note, of course. This note, F, is the root of the tonic chord (I) and also the fifth of the subdominant chord (IV), thus being a "common" note for these two chords which can thus be used to harmonize the melody as a whole. This aspect of melody harmonization will be explored further in Chapter 6.

You are now ready to perform "Lovely Evening" as a three-part round. Listen carefully to the other two parts as you sing your part, working for good intonation and tonal blend.

CHORDING WITH I, IV, AND V₇

With three chords at your disposal you will be able to provide accompaniments to many well-known songs. The five following are representative of the many types of songs that can be harmonized with the I, IV, and V₇ chords. We have limited ourselves to the keys C, F, and G because these are the only major keys available on the twelve-bar Autoharp. Songs in other keys are presented at the end of the chapter.

Chording with I, IV, and V₇ on the Autoharp. In singing and accompanying the songs, use the same procedure as before:

1. Establish the beat in an appropriate tempo.

2. Sing the song while conducting the beat.

3. Find the required chords on the Autoharp; remember the fingering positions for these: index finger on the I chord; middle finger on the V₇ chord; and fourth finger on the IV chord. Practice the chord changes I-IV-I-V₇-I until you can make them confidently.

4. Decide what style of chording is needed for the song at hand; then make up an appropriate accompaniment.

LAVENDER'S BLUE

2. Call up your men, dilly dilly, set them to work,
Some with a rake, dilly dilly, some with a fork;
Some to make hay, dilly dilly, some to thresh corn,
While you and I, dilly dilly, keep ourselves warm.

MICHAEL, ROW THE BOAT ASHORE

Moderato

Spiritual

REFRAIN

Mich - ael row the boat a - shore, Al - le - lu - ia,

Mich - ael row the boat a - shore, Al - le - lu - ia.

(Verses same tune as refrain)

1. Michael's boat's a music boat, Alleluia.
   Michael's boat's a music boat, Alleluia.

2. Sister, help to trim the sail, Alleluia.
   Sister, help to trim the sail, Alleluia.

3. Jordan's River is deep and wide, Alleluia.
   Meet my mother on the other side, Alleluia.

4. Jordan's River is chilly and cold, Alleluia.
   Kills the body but not the soul, Alleluia.

5. Gabriel, blow the trumpet horn, Alleluia.
   Blow the trumpet loud and long, Alleluia.

6. Brother, lend a helping hand, Alleluia.
   Brother, lend a helping hand, Alleluia.

7. Michael's boat's a gospel boat, Alleluia.
   Michael's boat's a gospel boat, Alleluia.

WHO WILL SHOE YOU FOOT?

With motion

Appalachian Song

Oh, who will shoe your pret - ty foot,

And who will glove your hand,

82

And who will kiss your ru - by red lips,

When I've gone to a for - eign land? _____

2. My pa will shoe my pretty foot,
My ma will glove my hand,
And none will kiss my ruby red lips,
Until Johnny comes home again.

3. I'm sure you know the crow is black,
And sometimes purple-blue,
If ever I prove false unto you
May I melt like the morning dew.

4. Till all the seas run dry, my love,
And rocks melt in the sun,
I'll love you till the day I die
And then you'll know that I'm done.

FOUR IN A BOAT

Briskly

Appalachian Folk Song

Four in a boat and the tide rolls high, Four in a boat and the tide rolls high;

Four in a boat and the tide rolls high, Get you a pret-ty one bye and bye.

2. Find your partner, stay all day,
We don't care what the old folks say.

3. Eight in a boat and it won't go round,
Swing that pretty one you just found.

OH, NO, JOHN

Moderately

English Folk Song

On yon-der hill there stands a creature, Who she is I do not know.

I'll go court her for her beau-ty; She must an-swer yes or no.

Oh, no, John, no, John, no, John, no.

2. Oh, madam, in your face is beauty!
   On your lips red roses glow;
   Will you take me for a lover?
   Madam, answer yes or no.

3. Oh, madam, I will give you jewels,
   I will make you rich and free;
   I will give you silken dresses;
   Madam, will you marry me?

4. Oh, madam, since you are so cruel,
   And since you do scorn me so,
   If I may not be your lover,
   Madam, will you let me go?

5. Then I will stay with you forever,
   If you will not be unkind;
   Madam, I have vowed to love you,
   Would you have me change my mind?

Chording with I, IV, and V₇ at the Piano. In making up piano accompaniments for these songs follow the same procedure as for the Autoharp. The only difference is that you must be able to make the chord changes easily and accurately so as not to destroy the rhythmic flow of the melody. This is how the chord changes are made at the piano:

Key of F

Key of G

The following two songs, "A-Hunting We Will Go" and "When the Saints Go Marching In," written out in full score, are to help the novice piano player acquire skill in playing melodies and three-chord accompaniments simultaneously. They can also serve as exercises in transposition of melodies and accompaniments to other keys. Try transposing them to at least two other keys.

A-HUNTING WE WILL GO

Oh a | hunt-ing we will | go,   a | hunt-ing we will | go.   We'll

catch a lit-tle fox and | put him in a box and | nev-er let him | go.

WHEN THE SAINTS GO MARCHING IN

Song from New Orleans

KEY SIGNATURES FOR MAJOR KEYS

Our experience thus far with major keys has been limited to the scales of C, F, and G. However, scales can be built on *any* tone on the keyboard and thus one may have many more choices of keys. The illustrations below of key signatures for sharp and flat keys show the possibility of fifteen different keys. Fortunately, only about nine of these keys are generally used for songs intended for use in the elementary grades. These are: C, G, D, A, E, F, Bb, Eb, and Ab. The reason for listing these keys in this particular order will become apparent from what follows.

Order of Sharps and Flats in Key Signatures. You already know that C major has no key signature, that the key signature for F major contains one flat (Bb) and that the key signature for G major contains one sharp (F#). Thus, the key having one flat more than C major has as its tonic a note which is a fifth *below* C (F), and the key having one sharp more than C major has for its tonic the note which is a fifth *above* C (G).

To find the keynote (tonic) for the key having two sharps in its signature we must count up five steps (a fifth) from G which would be D; for the key having three sharps in the signature we must count up a fifth from D which would be A; for keys with additional sharps we must proceed in the same manner. In other words, beginning with C major, *the "sharp" keys are arranged by ascending fifths adding one sharp to each successive key.*

MAJOR "SHARP" KEYS BY ASCENDING 5THS

For major scales having flats we must proceed in the opposite direction to find keys with additional flats in the key signature. Therefore, beginning with C major, *the "flat" keys are arranged by descending fifths adding one flat to each successive key.*

MAJOR "FLAT" KEYS BY DESCENDING 5THS

Check these sequences of keys on the piano to make sure that you understand the order in which sharps and flats occur in the key signatures. In musical notation the sharps and flats must always appear on the staff in this order.

87

Finding the Keynote from the Signature. It is important to learn to identify the key in which a song is written by its key signature. This you can do very quickly if you remember the following:

1. The sharp farthest to the right in a key signature is scale-tone 7 (*ti*). Count up to 8 (*do*) or down to 1 (*do*). The letter name of 8 or 1 is the name for that key.

2. The flat farthest to the right in the key signature is scale-tone 4 (*fa*). Count up or down to find 8 or 1, the letter name of which is the name of that key. A shortcut for identifying the key from signatures having two or more flats is: "The next to the last flat on the right is the keynote."

Test your ability to identify keys from the signature by writing in the keynote for the following key signatures in the treble clef. Then write the key signature and keynote for the same keys in the bass clef.

Example

PITCHING SONGS

To "pitch a song" is a common expression implying the establishment of the *tonality* (key feeling) and starting pitch (tone) of the melody. Songs usually begin and end on one of the tones of the tonic chord (I): 1-3-5 or *do-mi-so*.[2] Once the key in which the song is written has been ascertained from the key signature, the key feeling and beginning tone may be established in the following manner:

1. Sound the keynote, 1 or *do,* on a bell or piano.

2. Sing 1-3-5-3-1 or *do-mi-so-mi-do* to get the "feel" for the tonality.

3. Sing the initial pitch of the song.

For example:

When the song starts on *do*

do   do   mi   so   mi   do   do

[2] In minor keys the syllables would be *la-do-mi*. See Chapter 8, p. 139.

When the song starts on *mi*

do   do mi so mi do   mi

When the song starts on *so*

do   do mi so mi do   so

Try your skill in establishing the key feeling and beginning tone with some of the songs in this and preceding chapters. After gaining experience in pitching the songs in the keys indicated by their key signatures, transpose some of them and then establish the beginning pitch from the new key signatures in the same manner.

DEVELOPING SKILLS

SINGING

1. Sing the songs with syllable and number names.

2. Practice the appropriate conducting patterns as you sing the songs with words.

3. Sing the following sequences many times in various keys.

4. Using your knowledge of how to "pitch" songs, find the starting tones for "Shoo, Fly, Don't Bother Me," "Down in the Valley," "Lavender's Blue," and "Who Will Shoe Your Foot?"

PLAYING

1. Play all the melodies on the bells and on the piano.

2. Practice playing several of the songs on the piano with accompaniment.

3. Develop facility in playing the I-IV-I-V$_7$-I chord sequence in the keys of C, G, and F on the Autoharp.

4. Be able to build and play a major chord, 1-3-5 (*do-mi-so*), on any white or black key on the piano. Then learn to play the I-IV-I-V$_7$-I sequence from any of these chords.

READING

1. Establish the key note and starting pitch and then sing the following melodies with syllable and number names without the aid of an instrument.

Allegro moderato

Denmark

2. Clap or play on percussion instruments the melody-rhythms of the above melodies.

WRITING

1. Construct the major scales indicated by utilizing the major scale pattern and then extract the key signature, as in the example given.

Example:

A major

B-flat major

E major

A-flat major

2. Notate the chord progression I-IV-I-V₇-I in left-hand playing position in the keys indicated by the key signatures given.

The chord progression notation: I-IV-I-V$_7$-I

(A)

(B)

(C)

3. Transpose the first phrase of the following songs to the key indicated by the key signature.

LOVE SOMEBODY

FOUR IN A BOAT

UPWARD TRAIL

VOCABULARY

Be able to define or explain the following:

D.C. al Fine	tonality
dominant	tonic
key signature	transposition
order of sharps and flats in key signature	subdominant

ANALYTIC-CREATIVE ACTIVITIES

1. Transpose and play the following in the keys indicated.

WINTER ADE

Transpose to E, G, and B♭

OATS, PEAS, BEANS, AND BARLEY GROW

Transpose to D, F, and G

2. Sing and play "Polly Wolly Doodle" in parallel thirds and sixths by adding a second part above at the interval of a third and by adding a second part below at the interval of a sixth respectively. In the latter you will find the range of the second part too low for children to sing. What can you do to avoid this?

3. Try to improvise a second harmonizing part to "Down in the Valley" by ear.

4. Create rhythmic rounds similar to those presented in Chapter 3 (p. 66) using various meters: $\frac{3}{4}$, $\frac{4}{4}$, and $\frac{6}{8}$.

5. Study the melody to "Cradle Song" (p. 36). Why is this an example of a three-part song form (ABA)? How is the phrase structure of this song different from that of "Lightly Row?"

6. Study the separate phrases of these two melodies. Can you discover any repeated tonal or rhythmic patterns within a given phrase? (Repeated melodic or rhythmic patterns are called *motives*.) Are any of these patterns repeated sequentially or with variations?

7. Using the knowledge derived from the above analysis, compose a melody in three-part form.

5

Creating Parts to Songs

In this chapter we shall discuss a number of activities which can be introduced to add variety to musical experiences. These activities can also be used to provide individuals and small groups special opportunities for extending and enriching their contacts with music.

INTRODUCTIONS AND CODAS

An introduction may be used to establish the tonality or key feeling of a song to help the singer begin on the proper pitch, and it may be used to establish the beat, the tempo, and the mood of the song as well.

Introductions used merely for establishing tonality are quite simple: all that is needed is to play the I-V$_7$-I chord pattern on the Autoharp or piano in the key in which the song is to be sung. If the song is a three-chord song, the I-IV-I-V$_7$-I progression might be played.

Introductions for establishing tempo and mood are usually more extended. Such introductions are often based on some part or section of the song itself; for example, the final phrase of a song played on a melody instrument (or sung on a neutral syllable) with the accompaniment often makes a fitting introduction. This type of introduction would be appropriate for songs like "Cradle Song" (p. 36) and "Billy Boy" (p. 28).

CRADLE SONG

BILLY BOY

After you have tried these, look at some of the other songs to see if they lend themselves to the same kind of introductions.

Another form of introduction may consist of a repeated melodic motive, a distinctive rhythmic motive, a simple scale passage, or a combination of these. Here are several possibilities for an introduction to the round "White Coral Bells" (p. 31).

An introduction to "Rosa, Come and Go Dancing" (p. 35) might be something like this:

Sometimes an instrumental introduction of a more extended nature can be very effective. Let us use "Trot, Pony, Trot" as an example.

TROT, PONY, TROT

Chinese Folk Song

Moderately

Trot, trot, po - ny trot! Trot to Grand -ma's gate - way.

She'll come out and call her dog, And then we'll ride on jog - a - jog,

Trot, trot po - ny trot! Trot, trot po - ny trot!

96

This song has an obvious "Chinese" quality and the introduction should contribute to this feeling. If you have a Chinese gong and temple blocks available, the introduction might take this form:

After this eight-measure introduction the singing would begin and all the instruments, except the gong, would continue their two-measure patterns throughout the song.

Some songs can be made more interesting by the addition of a *coda* (ending section) which has the effect of sustaining the mood of the song a little longer and thus giving it a less abrupt ending.

Many codas consist merely of a repetition of the last phrase, or part of the last phrase, of the song with appropriate changes in tempo (usually slower) and in loudness (usually softer). An effective coda to "Merrily We Roll Along" (p. 78) would be a repetition of the last two measures, once or twice, sounding gradually softer and softer to the end. A similar "fading away" effect (*decrescendo*) might be created with "Du, Du, Liegst mir im Herzen" (p. 22) by repeating the last phrase softer and in a decreasing tempo (*ritardando*). For songs such as "Trot, Pony, Trot" one might use the introduction in reverse order for the coda. At the conclusion of the song, the instruments would continue playing, but with one instrument dropping out in turn every two measures and finally ending up with just a soft stroke of the gong. Try this.

Endless possibilities exist for adding simple but interesting introductions and codas to "dress up" many of the songs which you may encounter. However, not all songs lend themselves to such treatment, so do not overwork these ideas. Introductions and codas should be used only when they can make a distinct contribution to the over-all effect of the song.

CHANTS AND OSTINATI

An *ostinato* is a recurring rhythmic or melodic pattern (figure or motive) used as an accompaniment for a song. When such a pattern is played by an instrument, the term ostinato is usually used, but when words are added or replace the instrument, the term *chant* is used.

The reasons for adding chants and ostinati to songs are: (1) to increase interest and enjoyment; (2) to stimulate creative processes; (3) to extend rhythmic experiences; (4) to provide something that many out-of-tune singers can do with satisfaction; and (5) to develop independence in a type of part-singing that prepares for more advanced part-singing later on.

Chants and Ostinati for I Chord Tunes. It is easy to create a chant or ostinato to melodies which can be harmonized with only the I chord by basing it on the chord-root (1 or *do*). An example of this is the chant provided for "Little Tom Tinker," a melody that can be harmonized in its entirety with only the I chord. The chant is made up of two rhythmic motives taken

from the song (♩♪♩♪♩♪♩♪♩♪ and ♩ ♪♩ ♪), and the words attached to it are a logical comment on what is happening to little Tom:

LITTLE TOM TINKER

98

he be - gan to cry _____ Ma _____

Lit - tle Tom Tink - er be - gan to cry. Lit - tle Tom Tink - er be -

Ma _____ What a poor fel - low am I _____

gan to cry. Lit - tle Tom Tink - er be - gan to cry.

Practice the chant as you conduct the beat (fast $\frac{6}{8}$ meter). Next, divide the class into two groups, one of melody-singers and one of chanters, and sing the two parts together.

Chants such as this one are really more rhythmic than melodic, i.e., they have no melody—only one chanted pitch, and can therefore be played on a suitable percussion instrument equally as well. Try this.

An introduction to "Little Tom Tinker" can be created by having the chanters sing their pattern twice (four measures) before the melody singers enter. And at the end of the song the chanters can continue for another four measures to form a coda.

Scale-line chants and ostinati can also be very effective. An example of this is the following motive for "Little Tom Tinker." It has been transposed to the key of Eb so that the chanters will not have to sing too low.

Tom - my Tink - er

Another suggestion is to sing it as a two-part round plus the chant. With the addition of the introduction and the coda you will find that this song presentation becomes something of a "winding up" and "unwinding" process which makes it seem quite important!

Still more can be done by adding to the chant on scale tone 1 the same chant on 3, then adding another (all with the same words) on 5. As these parts are added, you find the chant sounding in three parts (1-3-5 chord tones). With the addition of the melody, a simple form of four-part singing results. Try this.

Here is another well-known round, the melody of which can be harmonized with only the I chord.

ARE YOU SLEEPING?

Among the chants and ostinati possible for this song are:

Note that scale tone 6 (D) sounds good even though it is not a chord tone.

Other songs which can be harmonized with the I chord only are "Good-bye, Ol' Paint" (p. 29), "Short'nin' Bread" (p. 32), "Row, Row, Row Your Boat" (p. 34), and "Old Chisholm Trail" (p. 167). Try creating chants and ostinati for these.

Chants and Ostinati for I-V₇ Chord Tunes. Chants can be improvised for songs which are harmonized with both the I and V₇ chords by using scale tone 5 throughout the song, except at the end, perhaps, where scale tone 1 may be needed to give the chant an appropriate ending. You will recall that scale tone 5 is common to both the I and V₇ chords:

Therefore, a chant based on this tone is bound to harmonize with either chord. Such chants are of the same type as those used for I chord tunes. For example, a chant for "Sandy Land" would be based on C (5) which is the common tone for the F (I) and C₇ (V₇) chords:

Sand - y land, Sand - y land

SANDY LAND

Lively

Play-Party Song

Make my liv-ing in sand - y land, Make my liv-ing in sand - y land

Make my liv-ing in sand - y land, Ladies, fare you well.

Some two-chord songs have a harmonic pattern which is repeated throughout the song. "Three Blind Mice" is one of these.

THREE BLIND MICE

Three blind mice,____ Three blind mice,____
See how they run!____ See how they run!____ They
all ran af-ter the farm-er's wife, She cut off their tails with a carv-ing knife, Did you
ev - er see such a sight in your life as three blind mice?____

Note that the harmonic pattern C-G$_7$-C (I-V$_7$-I) is repeated every two measures, and to create an ostinato for this song you must choose chord tones that fit this pattern. As you examine this chord progression, you will discover the possibility of two ostinati (1 and 2) and also that these might be combined into a two-part ostinato (3) made up of parallel thirds.

Try all three of these ostinati.

Other songs with repeated harmonic patterns are "Grandma Grunts" (p. 38) and "Go In and Out the Window" (p. 166). Make up ostinati for these.

You have already used scale tone 6 in chants for "Little Tom Tinker" (p. 98) and "Are You Sleeping?" (p. 100) quite effectively. This non-chord tone has the unique property of blending nicely with both the I and V₇ chords, and it is very useful in creating chants for certain types of songs. Thus, the tone figure 5-6-5 makes an interesting chant for "Skip to My Lou."

SKIP TO MY LOU

Fly in the but-ter-milk Shoo fly shoo, Fly in the but-ter-milk Shoo fly shoo,

Fly in the but-ter-milk Shoo fly shoo, Skip to my Lou my Dar - ling.

Lou, Lou skip to my Lou, Lou, Lou skip to my Lou,

Lou, Lou skip to my Lou, Skip to my Lou my dar - ling.

After learning the song, add this "5-6-5" chant:

Fly in the but-ter-milk shoo fly shoo   Fly in the but-ter-milk shoo fly shoo

Skip to my Lou ___   skip to my Lou ___   Skip to my Lou ___   skip to my Lou ___

To add variety to the final two measures or to a coda, try:

Skip to my Lou my dar - ling

Chants are sometimes made more enjoyable (and more effective) when the chanters stop singing for a few measures and then begin again, rather than sing the chant through the entire song. You may wish to experiment with this idea when a chant becomes monotonous.

Here is a song based on the old tune "Oh Bury Me Not on the Lone Prairie."

OLD TEXAS

I'm goin' to leave _____ old __Tex - as now _____ They've got no

use _____ for the long horn cow _____ They've plowed and fenced ____ my __cat- tle

range _____ and the peo - ple there _____ are __ all so strange _____

Sing it through several times while conducting or clapping the beats. As you sing, be sure to sustain the long notes (♩) which are *tied* over to connecting short notes (♩♩). After that add an accompaniment with the Autoharp and piano. Next, add a chant on 5 and 6, on the words "Leavin' Old Texas." Finally, imitate the "ridin' along" or "joggin' along" of the cowboy on his horse with percussion instruments on the rhythmic pattern. Here is how it would look:

OLD TEXAS

I'm goin' to

Leav-in' old Tex-as Leav-in' old Tex-as   Leav-in' old Tex-as Leav-in' old Tex-as

leave _____ old_Tex-as   now _____ They've got no

Leav-in' old Tex-as Leav-in'old Tex-as   Leav-in' old Tex-as Leav-in' old Tex-as

Begin with an introduction and end with a coda.

Still another idea for "Old Texas" is to make a two-part round out of it.
When you do this, leave out the chording.

I'm goin' to   leave _____ old_Tex-as   now_____ They're got no

I'm goin' to leave _____ old_Tex-as now

After you have mastered singing the song as a round, try adding the chant
and the percussion instruments. You now have a song with three different
parts being sung at one time, combined with a rhythmic accompaniment for
good measure—a real accomplishment indeed, which means that you are
growing in musical powers!

Sometimes a short section of a melody can be used as an ostinato. Analyze the harmonization of "Did You Ever See a Lassie?" Does it have a distinctive chord pattern? Could measures 9 and 10 ("this way and that way") be used as an ostinato throughout the song? Try this. If this should become monotonous, what might you do to remedy it?

DID YOU EVER SEE A LASSIE?

Other easy ways to improvise parts to a song include (1) singing the chord roots of the harmonization and (2) singing the chords in three parts instead of playing them on the Autoharp or piano. (Vocal and instrumental chording may, of course, be combined whenever this seems desirable.)

Singing Chord Roots. An effective accompaniment to a song can be created by having part of the class sing the chord roots, i.e. the note designated by the chord name. In the key of F, for example, the F chord designation indicates that the note F should be sung and the C₇ chord designation indicates that the note C should be sung. One might harmonize "Merrily We Roll Along" (p. 78) in the following manner:

MERRILY WE ROLL ALONG

Chord roots may be sung with a neutral syllable such as "la" or with words which fit the rhythm of the melody.

Learning to hear such chord changes "in your head" is valuable ear training, and you should practice singing chord roots to many of the songs in this book.

Singing Chords in Parts. Singing the designated chords in three parts is very effective with some songs. "Down in the Valley" (p. 76) lends itself beautifully to this type of vocal chording. Before singing the chords, write the chord progression needed in the proper key on the chalkboard and listen

---

[1] The suggestions given here for *vocal chording* can be adapted to instruments as well: a cello or a trombone might be used for playing chord roots; Resonator Bells could be used both for chord roots and for playing the complete chord.

to this as it is played on the piano. Next, divide the class into three groups
and practice singing the chords with a neutral syllable in this manner:

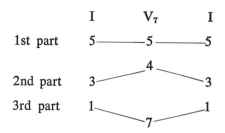

You may add a fourth part (bass part) by singing the proper chord root
with each chord. This is how such an arrangement of "Down in the Valley"
would look in notation:

etc.

This type of vocal chording can be very effective with the next two songs.
After you have learned the melody well, add the other parts following the
procedure suggested above.

RED RIVER VALLEY

sun- shine _____ that bright - ened our path - way a - while. _____
val - ley _____ and the girl who has loved you so true. _____

2. Won't you think of the valley you're leaving?
   Oh, how lonely, how sad it will be!
   Oh, think of the fond heart you're breaking,
   And the grief you are causing me to see!

LULLABY

Johannes Brahms

Lul - la - by and Good - night, with _____ Ros - es be - dight _____

with _____ Lil - lies o'er _____ spread is _____ ba - by's wee bed;

Lay thee down now and rest, may thy slum - ber be blest

Lay thee down now and rest may thy slum - ber be blest

6

Expressive Singing

In Chapter 1 you were advised to listen carefully to pitches so that you might reproduce them accurately with your singing voice, to work toward producing a natural-sounding voice revealing no strain or discomfort, to plan your breathing during singing to avoid breaking up the musical phrase, and to remember that singing is only sustained speech in which consonants are ordinarily a form of brief punctuation separating vowels. In this chapter we will relate some of these aspects to learning to sing more expressively.

To learn to sing expressively you must know the meaning of words and project this meaning when you sing. Give your full imagination and concentration to the message of the song and let your voice reflect its dramatic impact—the emotion and the mood—as you sing.

It often helps to *speak* the song before attempting to sing it, observing the natural stress of some of the words and the build-up of tensions and their release. Observe the pitch of a good speaking voice; it rises and falls in order to dramatize this tension and release in its success in conveying the message of the spoken words. Observe word phrases also; take breaths ordinarily at the end of these phrases. You do not break a phrase (or thought) by breathing during it when you speak; neither should you do this when you sing. Periods, commas, semi-colons, and notated rests assist in pointing out possible places to breathe. Apply this knowledge to singing the following songs. Study the musical phrases, the thoughts expressed in the poetry, and the punctuation of both the words and the music to determine the best places to take breaths.

MUSCLE ACTIVITY AND POSTURE

To permit your voice to sound its best there must be freedom of muscle activity of the tongue, lips, throat, neck, chest, and diaphragm. The tongue should be free and relaxed; the jaw is dropped down and the mouth is opened without tension. Thinking of a yawn helps to open and relax the throat. Diaphragmatic action is extremely important. This large muscle which separates the lung area from the abdominal area acts somewhat like a bellows which draws air into the lower lungs. Proper breathing makes full use of the capacity of this area. To feel the correct way to breathe bend over, place the hands at the waist with thumbs toward the back, and breathe. You should feel the diaphragm at work. Now stand erect and continue this same type of breathing. If you cough or laugh, you can feel the diaphragm move. Breathiness results when the singer uses his breath too rapidly. Practice releasing the breath slowly by blowing through a straw into a glass of water and by experimenting with releasing the breath very slowly between nearly closed lips, making no sound. When you stand, the weight of your body should rest on the balls of the feet. Stand as erect as possible. When you are seated, your posture from the waist up should be approximately the same as when you were standing.

BENDEMEER'S STREAM

Thomas More

Moderately

Irish Folk Melody

1. There's a bow - er of ro - ses by Ben - de-meer's stream,
In the time of my child - hood 'twas like a sweet dream,

And the night - in - gale sings round it all the day long,
To___ sit in the ro - ses and hear the bird's song.

That bow'r and its mu - sic I'll nev - er for - get,

But oft when a - lone in the bloom of the year,

I think is the night - in - gale sing - ing there yet,

Are the ro - ses still bright by the calm Ben - de - meer?

RANGE, RESONANCE, AND QUALITY

Higher pitches should normally have a lighter quality than lower pitches. Keep the voice free from tension and strain; think *high* when singing low, and think *low* when singing high. Ability to sing in the range of children's voices is important to those who plan to work with this age group. Thus the range of the adult voice should be expanded gradually to at least the following normal range for children:

The adult male voice would be one octave lower.

The cavities of the chest, pharynx, mouth, and head provide resonating chambers which can add resonance to voices. To gain a concept of this practice humming; then try to retain that sensation when singing. (Women should not attempt humming pitches higher than those shown above because the voice becomes pinched.)

The quality of the singing voice is governed in part by the words of songs and the moods projected by them, the correct quality being generally that which best communicates the message. The tone quality desirable for singing a lullaby is different from that for singing a stirring patriotic air, although dynamics and stylistic elements enter into this also. It is advisable to listen to recordings of singers who are acknowledged to possess superior voices.

Sing the following song with range, resonance, and quality in mind.

THE RIDDLE SONG

American Folk Song

has   no   end,   I   gave my love   a   ba - by   that's   not   cry - in'.
has   no   end? How   can there be   a   ba - by   that's   not   cry - in'.

3. A cherry when it's blooming it has no stone,
   A chicken when it's peepin' it has no bone,
   A ring when it's a rollin' it has no end,
   A baby when it's sleepin' is not cryin'.

DICTION

When one speaks, words and syllables are not separated; they are logically connected. The syllabication of words in dictionaries is not always a dependable indication of the way we pronounce word syllables. In singing, a general rule is to sustain the vowel as long as possible regardless of a possible contrary syllabication of the printed word beneath the notes. For example, the word clarinet is *clar-i-net* in the dictionary, but it is sung *cla-ri-net*.

Consonants should be articulated very rapidly, with few exceptions. The sibilant *s* must be pronounced with extreme brevity to avoid an unwelcome hissing sound. Be sure to sound final consonants of words; omitting them is a common fault of singers. For example, one often hears "silen' nigh' " instead of "silent night," and "an" instead of "and." As one teacher says, "Sound your *d*'s and cross your *t*'s." The consonant *r* can be troublesome; it has an ugly sound if sustained. In singing it is often sounded only very slightly, as in the word error: *ehruh - (r)* or very briefly as in the word world: *wuh - (r)ld*. Double consonants are pronounced as one; the dictionary syllabicates the word falling as fal-ling but we speak it and sing it as *faw-ling*. The same thing occurs with double consonants formed by adjacent words such as "and day." We pronounce this *"an-day."*

Because of the importance of vowels your teacher may suggest some vocal exercises consisting entirely of vowels. With the exception of the vowel sound *e* (as in Edward) and the vowel sound *ä* (as in are) vowels have two sounds, rather than one. For example, away is pronounced *uh-ooáy*, and beauty is pronounced *bióo-ty*. In the word day we find the diphthong *ā(ee)*. Old contains the diphthong *óh(oo)* and view reveals *u* pronounced as *(ee)óo*. *Ou* as in now is pronounced *áh(oo)* and the *oi* sound is joy is *óh(i)*. Dew is pronounced *(di)óo*, with the *di* only a brief introduction to the important *oo* sound.

Practice the following songs to apply principles of diction, posture, fluency, range, resonance, and expressiveness as discussed above.

FOR THE BEAUTY OF THE EARTH

2. For the wonder of each hour,
Of the day and of the night,
Hill and vale, and tree and flow'r
Sun and moon, and stars of light;
Lord of all, to Thee we raise
This our hymn of grateful praise.

3. For the joy of human love,
Brother, sister, parent, child,
Friends on earth and friends above,
For all gentle thoughts and mild;
Lord of all, to Thee we raise
This our hymn of grateful praise.

SHENANDOAH

2. Oh, Shenandoah, I love your daughter,
   Away, you rolling river.
   Oh, Shenandoah, I love your daughter,
   Away, we're bound away,
   'Cross the wide Missouri.

3. Oh, Shenandoah, I long to hear you,
   Away, you rolling river,
   Oh, Shenandoah, I'll not deceive you,
   Away, we're bound away,
   'Cross the wide Missouri.

SINGING IN PARTS

The study of expressive singing inevitably leads to part singing because the addition of parts tends to increase the possibilities of emotional impact as well as personal enjoyment. You have already had some experience in singing in parts in the form of rounds, chants, and vocal chording.

Singing Rounds. When rounds are sung, everyone sings the same part, but at different times. The main challenge is to enter at the proper time, to hear the other parts as you sing yours, and to achieve the proper balance of all parts. The following two rounds are slightly more demanding than the ones you have sung previously. Practice singing the first one for its expressive qualities. The second one provides an opportunity for a little "fun making."

DONA NOBIS PACEM

Three-Part Round

Pronounced: *doh-nah noh-bees pa-chèm* (or *pa-kem*)

"The Orchestra" can be sung as a round in the usual manner with each new part starting when the previous part begins with a new "instrument." It can also be sung as a "cumulative" song in the following manner: (1) Violin; (2) Clarinet; (3) Violin and Clarinet; (4) Trumpet; (5) Violin, Clarinet, and Trumpet; (6) Horn; (7) Violin, Clarinet, Trumpet, and Horn; (8) Drum; (9) Violin, Clarinet, Trumpet, Horn, and Drum. You will have fun working this out!

THE ORCHESTRA

Old Quodlibed

Moderato

Five-Part Round

The vi - o - lin's ring - ing like

The clar - i - net, the clar - i - net makes

The trump - et is sound - ing, ta - ta - ta -

The horn, the horn a -

The drum's play - ing two tones and

love - ly___ sing - ing, The vi - o - lin's

doo-dle, doo-dle, doo-dle, doo-dle det, The clar-i-net, the

ta - ta-te-ta, ta-ta-ta - ta-ta-te-ta, The trump - et is

wakes me at morn, The horn, the

al - ways the same tones, Five, one, one,

ring - ing like love - ly___ song.

clar-i-net makes doo - dle, doo-dle, doo-dle det.

sound - ing, ta - ta-ta - ta-ta-te-ta, ta-ta-ta - ta.

horn a - wakes me at morn.

five, five, five, five, five, one.

Singing Descants. A *descant* is an independent melody composed especially to accompany another melody. Singing songs with descants differs from singing rounds in that there are two different melodies going on at the same time, whereas in a round the same melody is sung by each part. The song should always be learned thoroughly before the descant is added. Descants can also be effective when played on an instrument such as bells, flute, or violin.

FAIR IS THE SUMMER

2. Beneath the rose-bush within the shade
   Fair is the summer,
   There lay, deep in dreams, a fairy maid.
   Fair is the summer.

3. What glitters there like to shining gold?
   Fair is the summer.
   'Tis bright curly locks a face enfold.
   Fair is the summer.

THE ASHGROVE

Singing Two-Part Music. Part-singing requires that the singer be aware of the other part or parts at all times and make his part harmonize or blend with the others so that they will be in tune. To begin with we suggest that you learn the melody very well, and with a good harmonic background. The new part can then be added in a way that helps you to hear the relationship of this part to the melody and the harmony. This may be done in several ways, one of which is to have the class hum the melody softly while listening to the teacher sing the new part or play it on the piano or the bells. After hearing the new part in relation to the melody, students who believe they can sing it along with the teacher or the instrument should do so, while the rest of the class continues to hum or sing the melody. In this way part-singing can be learned in a manner that adds to the understanding of the music as a *whole*. There are many different ways of stressing the relationship of each part to the other, and these might eventually include the entire class singing the new part while the teacher plays the melody on the piano or the bells. This same principle can be applied to the learning of descants. Later on as you become aware of the interval or chord relationship of the parts you will be able to read more than one part at a time.

The simplest two-part songs to begin with are those in which the parts move along together in thirds and/or sixths. However, after a little practice you will have no difficulty with other interval relationships.

Isaac Watts
Allegro

JOY TO THE WORLD

George Frederick Handel

Joy to the world! The Lord is come;

Let earth re - ceive her King;

Let ev - 'ry heart pre - pare him room

and heav'n and na - ture sing, and heav'n and na - ture sing

and heav'n and heav'n and na - ture sing.

BATTLE HYMN OF THE REPUBLIC

Julia Ward Howe

Civil War Song

Martiale

Mine eyes have seen the glo-ry of the com-ing of the Lord; He is
tramp-ling out the vint-age where the grapes of wrath are stor'd; He hath
loos'd the fate-ful light-ning of His ter-ri-ble swift sword; His
truth is march-ing on. Glo-ry glo-ry hal-le-

CHORUS

lu-jah! Glo-ry glo-ry hal-le-lu-jah!

Glo-ry glo-ry hal-le-lu-jah! His truth is march-ing on.

2. I have seen Him in the watchfires of a hundred circling camps,
They have builded Him an altar in the ev'ning dews and damps;
I can read His righteous sentence by the dim and flaring lamps:
His day is marching on.
REFRAIN
Glory glory hallelujah! Glory glory hallelujah!
Glory glory hallelujah! His truth is marching on.

3. In the beauty of the lilies Christ was born across the sea,
With a glory in His bosom that transfigures you and me.
As He died to make men holy, let us die to make men free,
While God is marching on.
REFRAIN
Glory glory hallelujah! Glory glory hallelujah!
Glory glory hallelujah! His truth is marching on.

121

CHILDREN'S PRAYER

Adelheid Wette

Andante

Engelbert Humperdinck

When at night I go to sleep,— Four-teen an - gels watch do— keep,

Two my head are guard - ing, Two my feet are guid - ing

Two are on my right hand, Two are on my left hand,

Two are on my right hand, Two are on my—

Two who warm-ly cov - er, Two who o'er me hov - er

left hand Two who warm-ly cov - er, Two who o'er me

cresc.

Two to whom tis giv - en To guide my steps to Hea - ven.

hov - er, Two who guide my steps to Hea - ven.

Singing Three-Part Music. Three-part music provides further opportunities for expressive singing. Classes experienced in singing two-part music usually have no difficulty in adding another part.

The easiest three-part songs are those in which the three parts move together. You will soon discover that a great deal of three-part music is based on the chords with which you are familiar by now. At first, you may wish to add one part at a time to the melody. However, if you are good readers, you may be able to sing all the parts together from the start.

JACOB'S LADDER

MORNING PRAISE

Author Unknown

Andante

Ludwig Van Beethoven

Love is to hu - man hearts What sun-shine is to flow'rs

And friend-ship is the fair - est thing In this great world of ours.

STARS OF THE SUMMER NIGHT

Henry W. Longfellow

Dolce

J. B. Woodbury

Stars of the sum-mer night, Far in you az - ure deeps,

Hide, hide your gold - en light, She sleeps, my la - dy sleeps;

She sleeps, She sleeps, my la - dy sleeps.

Singing Four-Part Music. College classes which include men might enjoy singing the following four-part songs arranged for soprano, alto, tenor, and bass. The patriotic songs in Appendix C may also be sung in four parts.

RESPONSE AFTER PRAYER

George Whelpton

Hear our prayer, O Lord, Hear our prayer, O Lord;

In - cline Thine ear to us, and grant us Thy peace. A - men.

AULD LANG SYNE

Robert Burns

Scotch Air

Should auld ac-quaint-ance be for-got, And nev - er bro't to mind?
And here's a hand, my trust - y frien'. And gie's a hand o' thine;

Should auld ac-quaint-ance be for-got, And days of auld lang syne?
We'll tak' a cup o' kind-ness yet, For auld__ lang__ syne?

REFRAIN

For auld__ lang__ syne, my dear, For auld__ lang__ syne;

We'll tak' a cup o' kind-ness yet For__ auld__ lang__ syne.

7

The Pentatonic Scale and the Modes

Our musical experiences have thus far been confined to the tonality with which we are most familiar, that based on the major scale. We shall now explore other scales and some of the music resulting from them.

THE PENTATONIC SCALE

The term "scale" means "ladder" and denotes a series of rising pitches. One of the most interesting scales is the *pentatonic* or five-tone scale. It is considered to be important historically as the prototype of all scales, and it is found all over the world.

The black keys on the piano exemplify the pentatonic scale.

Since each black key has two pitch-names, this scale can be notated in the following manner, also:

1 2 3 4 5 (1)

Play this scale on the bells or piano ascending and descending. As you do this, you will discover that it seems to lack any strong feeling of a tonal center as compared with the major scale. The reason for this is that the pentatonic scale contains no half steps. The writer of pentatonic tunes can choose whichever of the five pitches he desires as the tonic and begin his scale on that pitch. In the following song the tonic chosen is E♭.

LAND OF THE SILVER BIRCH

Rhythmically

Ontario Folk Song

Land of the sil - ver birch, home of the bea - ver,

Where still the might - y moose wan - ders at will;

Blue lake and rock - y shore, I will re - turn once more

Boom de de boom boom, Boom de de boom boom Boom de de boom boom boom.

Because any one of the five tones may be selected as the tonic, this scale might appear in five different forms. One frequently utilized to help the

128

student remember the scale tones is that which is like the major scale with steps 4 and 7 removed.

Note that the interval pattern for this form of the scale is:

1	2	3	4	5	(1)
whole step	whole step	1½ steps	whole step	1½ steps	

SYLLABLES FOR PENTATONIC SCALES

The pentatonic scale appears on white keys as follows:

The first one is clearly suggestive of the key of C, the second the key of F, and the third the key of G. We have inserted the key signatures for the scales beginning on F and G because this is usually done when pentatonic melodies appear in notation.

When syllables are used with pentatonic scales, they are related to the key signature as they are with major scales. Sung with syllables the above pentatonic scales built on C, F, and G would all be:

do   re   mi   so   la   (do)

Sing these scales several times with syllables. Also sing the major scale and the pentatonic scale beginning on the same pitch alternately to get the feel of the similarity and difference between the two kinds of scales. Next, try to read "Young Man Who Wouldn't Hoe Corn" with syllables unaided by an instrument.

129

YOUNG MAN WHO WOULDN'T HOE CORN

Moderately

American Folk Song

I'll sing you a song and it's not ver-y long,

It's a-bout a young man who would-n't hoe corn;

The rea-son why, I can't tell,

For this young man was al-ways well

Many of our familiar folk songs are based on the pentatonic mode, for example, "Auld Lang Syne," "Old McDonald Had a Farm," "Get on Board, Little Children," "Swing Low, Swing Chariot," and "The Campbells Are Coming." Prove this to yourself by playing these tunes on the black keys of the bells or piano.

THE MODES

When the term *mode* is used today in relation to scales, it is most likely to refer to those six which evolved through Hebrew, Greek, and Roman usage to become known eventually as the following: Ionian, Dorian, Phrygian, Lydian, Mixolydian, and Aeolian. They were used in the liturgical chants of certain religious groups, primarily the Roman Catholic Church. The Ionian mode is the major scale, and the Aeolian mode is the minor scale in natural form (see Chapter 8). Thus, it is the remaining four modes which are "different." Examine them to discover their distinguishing characteristics as compared to the major scale.

A sizeable number of folk songs is found to be modal. "Every Night When the Sun Goes In" is in the Mixolydian mode and "The Shanty Boys in the Pine" is in the Dorian mode.

EVERY NIGHT WHEN THE SUN GOES IN

American

Ev' - ry night_____ when the sun goes in,_____

Ev' - ry night_____ when the sun goes in,_____

Ev' - ry night_____ when the sun goes in,_____

I hang down my head_____ and mourn- ful cry._____

THE SHANTY BOYS IN THE PINE

Moderato

Lumberjack Song

Come all ye jol-ly shan-ty boys, come lis-ten to my song,___
The chop-pers and the saw-yers, they lay the tim-ber low.___

It's all a-bout the shan-ties and how they get a-long.___
The skid-ders and the swamp-ers, they hol-ler to and fro.___

They are a jol-ly crew of boys, so mer-ry and so fine,___
And then there come the load-ers, be-fore the break of day,___

Who while a-way the win-ters a cut-ting down the pine.___
Come load___ up the teams, boys, and to the woods a-way.___

3. The broken ice is floating, and sunny is the sky;
   Three hundred big and strong men are wanted on the drive.
   With cant hooks and with jampikes these noble men do go,
   And risk their lives each springtime on some big stream you know.

DEVELOPING SKILLS

SINGING

1. Sing "Land of the Silver Birch" as a two-part canon with the parts four measures apart.

2. Practice singing the pentatonic scales on p. 129 with syllables.

3. Practice singing and listening to the modes on p. 131.

PLAYING

1. Practice playing the pentatonic scale in the five forms. To do this, each form would begin on a different step of the scale. As you play them, identify the form which relates to the major scale; identify the form which relates to the minor scale.

2. Play the songs mentioned on p. 130 on the black keys of the piano or bells.

ANALYTIC-CREATIVE ACTIVITIES

1. Present a keyboard imitation of Indian drums by adding the following bourdon (drone bass) to "Land of the Silver Birch."

   The bourdon can appear in forms other than the "open fifth" version shown here. For example, the two notes could be played in alternation, and other notes within the pentatonic scale could be added. Try to change this bourdon after you have mastered it.

2. As an experiment, combine "Land of the Silver Birch" with "Trot, Pony, Trot" (p. 96). What did you learn from this?

3. Select one of the following songs: "Whistle, Daughter, Whistle" (p. 6), "Goodbye, Old Paint" (p. 29), "Short'nin' Bread" (p. 32), "Grandma Grunts" (p. 38) and "Li'l 'Liza Jane" (p. 42). Add to the selected song a type of bourdon similar to those used in No. 1 above. Invent a pentatonic vocal chant or instrumental ostinato, or both, to add to the melody and bourdon.

4. Improvise a composition by creating a bourdon, adding chants or ostinati above this; then improvise a melody above these parts.

5. Select one of the modes other than the Ionian and Aeolian and write a melody based upon it.

Minor Scales and Chording

Many of our favorite songs are in minor keys. The characteristic quality of the minor mode is evident in this Palestinian song of friendship:

SHALOM CHAVERIM

Moderato

Israeli Round

Sha - lom cha-ve-rim! Sha - lom cha-ve-rim! Sha - lom, sha -
Fare - well good friends, Fare - well, good friends Fare - well, fare -

lom! Le hit - ra - ot, le - hit - ra - ot, Sha -
well! Till we meet a - gain, till we meet a - gain, Fare -

lom, sha - lom!
well, fare - well!

* Pronounced: sha-lom khah-vay-reem

This beautiful song should be sung very expressively in legato style. Sing it as a three-part round also.

THE RELATIVE MINOR

From the key signature used for "Shalom Chaverim" you might have assumed that it was in F major, but your ear has already told you that this was not so. The explanation for this is that every minor scale shares a key signature with a major scale and begins on the sixth degree (*la*) of that scale. Major and minor keys which have the same key signature are said to be *relative*. Your concept of the key signature must now be broadened to include the fact that *for each key signature there are two related keys, one major and one minor*. Thus the key signature containing one flat (B♭) may indicate either F major or D minor.

The following illustrates how these two keys are related:

Sing these two scales with syllables several times, starting alternately on *do* and on *la*.[1] Also play them on the piano and on the bells.

The relative minor of a major scale may be determined by singing down to *la* (*do-ti-la*) which then becomes the home tone of the minor scale. Here are some examples:

The relative minor of G major is E minor.

The relative minor of C major is A minor.

Check your understanding of this principle by finding these scales on the piano and by building them with the Resonator Bells. Also practice singing them with syllables.

Could you transpose "Shalom Chaverim" to E minor? What would happen if you transposed it to A minor?

Number Names for Minor Scales. In the above examples we have used only syllable names for the minor scale degrees because the same syllable names

[1] The F major scale is the Ionian mode on F and the D minor scale is the Aeolian mode on D. See Chapter 7, p. 131.

are used for relative major and minor keys. However, when number names are used for minor scales, the 6 (*la*) of the major scale becomes the 1 (*tonic*) of its relative minor scale: [2]

F major

D minor

All chord designations in minor keys (I, IV, V₇, and others) are based upon this system of numbering the degrees of the minor scale, and we shall use it in what follows.

THE MINOR CHORD

Only one chord is needed to accompany "Shalom Chaverim." This is the chord marked "Dm" on the Autoharp. Find this chord, strum and listen to it a few times, then proceed to make up an appropriate accompaniment for this song.

In notation, the D-minor chord looks like this:

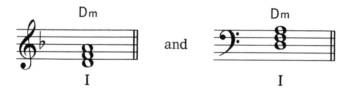

Note that this chord is made up of the 1-3-5 of the minor scale. The chord root is 1 (D) and it is therefore the I chord of D minor. Compare this chord with the I chord in D major by playing them on the piano:

D major   D minor

The D-major chord becomes a D-minor chord by lowering 3 one half step. The same letter names, D-F-A, are used for both chords and the 1-3-5 arrangement is unchanged. D is the tonic in both keys, and the difference in the quality of the two chords is a result of the key signatures which make 3 in the minor key one half step lower than it is in the major key.

On the piano the playing position for the I chord in D minor is the same as for D major.

---

[2] Some teachers prefer to think of the minor scale as beginning on 6 (*la*) and they utilize the major scale numbers when they sing the minor scale. Their reasoning is that the syllable names do not change when one sings them in minor keys, thus neither should the number names change. However, when chord numbers are used, they must think of the minor scale as beginning on "1."

"On My Journey Home" is another song in D minor, but it requires two chords, the I and IV chords, for the accompaniment. The IV chord becomes a minor chord in the minor key also.

Find the "Dm" and "Gm" buttons on the Autoharp and place the index finger on the first chord and the middle finger on the second. As you practice alternating these chords listen to the minor quality of this progression.

Use broad, relaxed strokes for your chording to this song; also try to preserve the long phrases as you sing the melody in a sustained legato style.

ON MY JOURNEY HOME

2. Should earth against my soul engage,
   And Satan's darts be hurled,
   Then I can smile at Satan's rage,
   And face a frowning world.

3. Let all cares like a deluge come,
   Let storms of sorrow fall,
   May I but safely reach my home,
   My God, my heaven, my all.

In playing the I-IV-I sequence in D minor on the piano we arrange the chord tones in the same as we did for D major:

THREE FORMS OF MINOR SCALES

In contrast to the major scale which is constructed on a single pattern of whole and half steps (see p. 70), there are three patterns of minor scales. These are the *natural,* the *harmonic,* and the *melodic* forms of the minor scale.

The Natural Minor. The two preceding songs were based on the natural form of the D minor scale. Let us compare this with the D major scale:

The difference between these two scales is in the arrangement of whole and half steps. In the major scale the half steps are between 3 and 4 and between 7 and 8, but in the natural minor the half steps occur between 2 and 3 and between 5 and 6. Play these scales on the piano and bells to make sure that you understand the difference between the two patterns.[3]

Review "Shalom Chaverim" and "On My Journey Home" and note that all the tones in these melodies belong to the natural form of the D minor scale.

"Pat Works on the Railway" is another song based on the natural form of the minor scale, in this case A minor. This key is relative to C major and has neither sharps nor flats in the key signature (see p. 135).

[3] Major and minor scales which have the same beginning note (*tonic*) are called *parallel,* and the minor scale is referred to as the *tonic* minor of the major.

Try to read this song with syllables or numbers without the aid of an instrument. Establish the tonality (key feeling) by sounding the keytone, *la,* on the piano or bells and then sing *la-do-me-do-la.* The song begins on the tonic.

la   do   mi   do   la   la

PAT WORKS ON THE RAILWAY

Vigorously

Irish American Song

In eight-een hun-dred and for-ty one, I put me cord'-roy breech-es on, I

put me cord'- roy breech-es on To work up-on the rail - way.

REFRAIN

Fil - le- me-oo - re - oo - re-ay,   Fil - le - me-oo - re - oo - re - ay,

Fil - le - me-oo - re - oo - re-ay,   To work up -on the rail - way.

2. In eighteen hundred and forty-two,
I did not know what I should do,
I left the auld world for the new
To work upon the railway.

3. In eighteen hundred and forty-three,
'Twas then I met sweet Biddy Magee,
And an illygant wife she's been to me
While workin' on the railway.

4. In eighteen hundred and forty-six,
They pelted me with stone and bricks,
Oh, I was in a awful fix
While workin' on the railway.

To accompany this song you will need three chords: the "Am" (I), the "Dm" (IV), and the "C" (III) chords.

Find these chords on the Autoharp and make up an appropriate accompaniment.

The III ("C") chord usually sounds best when it is played in root position, the position in which it is found on the Autoharp. We suggest that you use the following playing positions of the three chords for your piano accompaniment to this song:

The Harmonic Minor. Our next song is a familiar spiritual written in the key of D minor.

JOSHUA FOUGHT THE BATTLE OF JERICHO

140

Gid - e - on, You may talk a - bout your men of Saul, But there's

none like good old Josh - ua, At the bat - tle of Jer - i - cho.

2. Right up to the walls of Jericho,
   They marched with spear in hand,
   "Go blow them ram horns," Joshua cried,
   "Cause the battle is in my hand."

3. Then the lamb, ram, sheep horns began to blow,
   And the trumpets began to sound,
   Joshua told the children to shout that mornin',
   And the walls came tumblin' down.

As you sing this song and look at the notation you will discover a C♯ over the second syllable of "Josh-ua." Since there is no sharp in the key signature, this accidental requires explanation. The reason for this C♯ is that the melody of this song is based on the *harmonic* form of the D minor scale, whereas the two previous songs in this key were based on the natural form. Let us compare the two forms of the D minor scale.

Note that the seventh tone (7) of the natural minor scale has been raised one half step to change it into a harmonic minor. This creates an interval of a step and one-half (*augmented second*) between 6 and 7 (B to C♯) and this interval is the distinctive characteristic of the harmonic form of the minor scale. The raised 7 also creates a leading tone that has a strong pull toward 8. Such a leading tone is missing in the natural minor. Play both forms of this minor scale on the bells and piano several times to familiarize yourself with their distinctive qualities and so that you can identify them when you hear them. Also practice singing them, both ascending and descending.

For the accompaniment to "Joshua Fought the Battle of Jericho" we need only two chords, the I and V₇ chords in D minor. You are already familiar with the I chord in this key and know that it is a minor chord. Let us see what the V₇ chord looks like in the harmonic form of D minor:

If you compare this chord with the V₇ chord in D major, you will discover that it is the same chord that you have been using in this major key.

This would also be the case for all dominant seventh chords in major and minor keys which have the same tonic (begin on the same note): *the V₇ chords would be the same in both keys.*

The "Dm" and "A₇" chords are easy enough to find on the Autoharp and you have already used both of these chords previously on the piano for your song accompaniments. Notated in playing position for the piano they would look like this:

You will probably not experience any difficulty in making up an accompaniment to "Joshua Fought the Battle of Jericho" with the Autoharp. However, playing the melody *and* the accompaniment on the piano at the same time may cause some problems for the inexperienced pianist. Perhaps most of you will limit yourself to singing the melody and accompanying yourself with the chords indicated. An effective accompaniment can be created by playing the chord roots in the left hand and the treble-clef chords in the right hand, like this: [4]

[4] See Chapter 9, "Variety in Piano Chording."

Our next song, "Go Down, Moses," is in the key of A minor.

GO DOWN, MOSES

Negro Spiritual

When Is - rael was in E - gypt's land, Let my peo - ple go.
"Thus said the Lord," bold Mo - ses said, "Let my peo - ple go.
"No more shall they in bond - age toil; Let my peo - ple go.
"Your foes shall not be - fore you stand; Let my peo - ple go.

Op - pressed so hard they could not stand, Let my peo - ple go.
If not I'll smite your first-born dead. Let my peo - ple go."
Let them come out with E - gypt's spoil; Let my peo - ple go."
And you'll pos - sess fair Ca-naan's land; Let my peo - ple go."

REFRAIN

Go down, Mo - ses, Way down in E - gypt's land,

Tell ole Pha - raoh, Let my peo - ple go.

Notice the G♯ on the word "people" every time it occurs. This tells us that the melody to this song is based on the harmonic form of the A minor scales:

1 2 3 4 5 6 7 8
la ti do re mi fa si la

Three chords are required for the accompaniment: I, IV, and V₇ or "Am," "Dm" and "E₇."

143

Find these chords on the Autoharp and make up an accompaniment appropriate to the mood of this song. Here are the same chords arranged for the piano:

The Melodic Minor. The third form of the minor scale, the melodic minor, differs from the natural minor only in its *ascending* progression in which both 6 and 7 are raised one half step. However, the *descending* melodic minor scale is identical with the natural minor.

Sing this scale several times as you play it on the piano or bells until you get the feel of the difference in the ascending and descending patterns. Can you sense any similarity between the ascending melodic minor and the ascending major scale starting on the same tonic?

The "Welsh Fishers' Song" is an example of a melody based on the melodic minor.

WELSH FISHERS' SONG

We know that be - low, un-der break - er and swell,

Lie the mag - i - cal caves where the sea fair - ies dwell.

2. Far under the sea, where the green waters flow,
Fairies told the fish all the lore that they know.
They fed those fine fish to a wonderful size,
Come and buy them and eat them and learn to be wise.

For the accompaniment you would use the same chords that you utilized for "Go Down Moses." For variety in piano chording try one of the patterns suggested for $\frac{3}{4}$ meter in Chapter 9 (p. 162).

In conclusion, the three forms of the minor scale have one common characteristic: the half step between scale tones 2 and 3. The differences between the three forms are these:

The natural minor contains no accidentals.

The harmonic minor has a raised seventh degree.

The melodic minor has raised sixth and seventh degrees ascending; it is the same as the natural minor descending.

MIXING MINORS AND MAJORS

The use of two forms of the minor scale in the same song is exemplified in "Charlie Is My Darling," where the verse is in the melodic minor and the refrain is in the harmonic minor. The key is B minor and we have written it out in full score to assist you in playing it on the piano. Note that the chord designations, "Am," "C," "Dm," and "E₇" are for the Autoharp. The required chords for B minor are not available on this instrument and therefore the melody has to be transposed down one whole step when Autoharp accompaniment is used.

CHARLIE IS MY DARLING

Scottish Song

"When Johnny Comes Marching Home" is a good example of a lively song in the minor mode. It is also another interesting example of how a composer may use two forms of the minor scale, the natural and the harmonic, in the same piece of music.

This song is in A minor. Observe the G♮ in the third and fourth measures which indicates the natural form of this key, while the G♯ in the next to the last measure is a characteristic of the harmonic form of A minor. The harmonization of the melody supports this analysis. The use of "Am" (I) and "C" (III) in the first two phrases shows that this part of the melody is based on the natural form of A minor (see p. 140) and the chords "Am" (I), "Dm" (IV), and "E₇" (V₇) which are utilized in the last two phrases are the chords we have learned to associate with the harmonic form of this key (see p. 143).

WHEN JOHNNY COMES MARCHING HOME

Louis Lambert
(Patrick Gilmore)

When John- ny comes march - ing home a - gain, Hur - rah!____ Hur -

rah!____ We'll give him a hear - ty wel - come then, Hur -

rah!____ Hur - rah!____ The men will cheer,__ the

boys will shout, The la - dies, they__ will all turn out, And we'll

all feel gay when John - ny comes march - ing home.____

After you have reviewed the required chords, proceed to make up an accompaniment on the Autoharp. You will find that a rapid, crisp stroke will add rhythmic vitality to the singing of this song.

If you have the requisite pianistic facility, you may be able to play both melody and chords together. If not, use the following accompaniment for your singing (see Chapter 9 for other possibilities).

Occasionally relative major and minor keys may be used in the same song. Such is the case with "We Three Kings of Orient Are" in which the verse is in D minor and the refrain is in F major. You will recall that these two keys have the same key signature. A satisfactory piano accompaniment for this song will require the use of some new chords. A detailed explanation of these chords is given in Chapter 10 and you might like to look this over at this time. However, the chord designations in the music should enable you to accompany this song with the Autoharp very nicely.

WE THREE KINGS OF ORIENT ARE

"The Erie Canal" has a melody which alternates between D minor and F major, also. The melody begins in D minor, changes to F major in the third phrase, returns to D minor in the fourth phrase, and then changes to F major for the refrain. Such key changes are called *modulations,* and this melody modulates back and forth between D minor and F major.

For the accompaniment to "The Erie Canal" you will need the I-IV-V₇ chords in both F major ("F," "B♭," "C₇") and D minor ("Dm," "Gm," "A₇"). Find these chords on the piano and on the Autoharp and review the chord changes in each key. As you proceed to make up the accompaniment, observe that the last chord ("A₇") in the third measure over the word "hay" belongs to D minor, not to F major. A chord used in this manner in changing from one key to another is called a *modulating* chord. The last chord in the fourth phrase, the "C₇" over the fermata, serves as a modulating chord from D minor to F major. To help you with the piano accompaniment to this song we have notated it in full score.

THE ERIE CANAL

KEY SIGNATURES FOR MINOR KEYS

The simplest way to think about key signatures for minor keys is to relate them to the signatures for major keys. In Chapter 4 (p. 87) we provided charts showing in which order sharps and flats occur in major key signatures and we also explained how the keynote (tonic) could be determined from any given signature. You should review this part of the chapter at this point since complete familiarity with major key signatures is essential to determining key signatures for minor keys.

At the beginning of this chapter (p. 135) you learned that for each key signature there are two related keys, one major and one minor. Subsequently, you learned that every minor scale begins on the sixth degree (6) of some major scale. This gives you the cue for finding the keynote of a minor key from a given key signature:

1. Determine which major key the signature signifies.
2. Count up or down to the sixth degree of this scale (6). This is the tonic (keynote) of the minor key with the same key signature.

To test your understanding of this, notate the keynote for the minor keys indicated by the following signatures:

Major or Minor? You cannot decide whether a melody is in major or minor from the key signature alone. You must also examine the melody itself.

In Chapter 4 (p. 88) you learned that melodies in major keys usually begin and end on one of the tones of the tonic chord (I). This is also the case with melodies in minor keys. Consequently, one must look at the beginning note and/or the final note of a melody to determine whether it is in major or minor. If these tones belong to the:

> *do - mi - so* chord, the melody will be in major;
>
> *la - do - mi* chord, the melody will be in minor.

If you examine the songs in this chapter, you will see that they all begin on either *so* or *la* and that they all end on *la*.

To confirm your understanding of this, indicate which keys the following beginning and ending pitches of melodies signify:

Key: _____   _____   _____   _____   _____

Finally, as you come to the end of this chapter pertaining to minor scales and chording, review the following principles pertaining to major and minor scales at the keyboard:

1. Major and minor scales having the same key signature are *relative*.

2. Major and minor scales starting on the same tone are *tonic* or *parallel*.

3. Every minor scale begins on the sixth degree of some major scale.

4. The dominant seventh chord (V_7) is the same in both major and minor keys of the same name.

DEVELOPING SKILLS

SINGING

1. Sing the melodies with syllable and number names.

2. Practice the appropriate conducting patterns as you sing the songs with words.

3. Sing first the major scale and then its relative *natural* minor with syllables and numbers on D, E♭, F, and G.

4. Sing the natural, harmonic, and melodic forms of the minor scale with syllable and number names starting on B, C, and E.

5. Using your knowledge of how to "pitch" songs in minor keys (see p. 139), practice finding the starting tone for "Go Down Moses," "Welsh Fishers' Song," and "Charlie Is My Darling."

6. Sing the following sequences many times in the keys of E minor, D minor, C minor, and F minor.

153

PLAYING

1. Play all the melodies on the bells and on the piano.

2. Develop facility in playing the I-IV-I-V₇-I chord progression in the keys of A minor and D minor on the Autoharp.

3. Be able to build and play a minor chord, 1-3-5 (*la-do-mi*), on any white or black key on the piano. Then learn to play the I-IV-I-V₇-I chord progression from any of these chords.

4. Practice chording the songs on the Autoharp and piano to accompany your singing.

5. Practice playing several of the songs on the piano with the chord accompaniment.

READING

1. Find the keytone and starting pitch from the key signature and then sing the following melodies with syllable and number names without the aid of an instrument.

2. Establish a firm beat then clap or play on percussion instruments the following melody-rhythms taken from songs in this chapter. Can you identify the songs from which they were extracted?

WRITING

1. Write the minor scales indicated by the key signature. Show both ascending and descending forms of the melodic minor.

   Example

natural form   harmonic form

melodic form

natural form   harmonic form

melodic form

2. Notate the I-VI-I-V₇-I chord progression in major and minor keys having the *same tonic,* as in the example. Write in the proper key signatures for the keys indicated.

Example

C major

I   IV   I   V⁷   I

C minor

I   IV   I   V⁷   I

F major

F minor

E major

E minor

G major

G minor

VOCABULARY

Be able to explain the following terms:

augmented second   parallel minor
harmonic minor   relative minor
modulation   tonic minor
natural minor

ANALYTIC-CREATIVE ACTIVITIES

1. Transpose "Zum Gali Gali" to E minor and sing it in this key. Also create a percussion accompaniment for the singing with an introduction and a coda.

ZUM GALI GALI

[1] Pronounce: *a* as in father; *he* like hay; *le* with very short e; *i* as in machine; *o* as in come; *u* as in rule; *ch* as in German "ach."

An approximate translation of the various Hebrew phrases: 1. & 2. The pioneer's purpose is labor; 3. The pioneer is for his girl; 4. Peace for all the nations. A suggested English verse is "We will work till day-light is done; We will fight till freedom is won." The words "Zum gali gali" are probably meaningless.

158

A - vo - dah le 'man he - cha - lutz.

Zum ga - li ga - li ga - li, Zum ga - li ga - li.

2. Avodah le 'man hechalutz
   Hechalutz le man avodah.

3. Hechalutz le man hab'tulah;
   Hab'tulah le 'man hechalutz.

4. Hashalom le 'man ha'amim;
   Ha'amim le 'man hashalom.

2. "Discover" the harmonic form of the minor scale by adding a lower part at the interval of a third to the melody of "Zum Gali Gali." The final measure gives the clue to this. Both parts should end on the tonic.

3. Create a chant or ostinato to "Go Down Moses."

4. Add a lower part at the interval of a third to the refrain of "Erie Canal." Did this work out satisfactorily? If not, what changes could be made to obtain a two-part harmonization?

5. Are there any parts of "Joshua Fought the Battle of Jericho" to which one might add a second part? Where?

6. Compose a two-phrase melody based on the harmonic form of a minor scale. Harmonize the melody with the proper chords.

9

Variety in Piano Chording

Thus far your piano accompaniments have probably consisted largely of "block" chords, i.e. the three chord tones struck together at one time. In this chapter we will suggest ways in which you may create other types of accompaniments. Besides providing a harmonic background for the singing and playing of songs, accompaniments are used to establish the tempo, the style, the mood, and the expressiveness of various types of songs. The possibilities for creating different types of accompaniments are almost unlimited. After you have explored those which follow, you will be able to invent others on your own.

There are two kinds of chording commonly used for piano accompaniments: left-hand chording to accompany the melody played in the right hand and chording with both hands as the melody is being sung or played on another instrument. Block chords may be used in either case; however, "broken" chords in which the notes of the chords are separated and played in succession offer many additional possibilities for variety in piano accompaniments.

LEFT-HAND CHORDING

To begin with, play "Little Duckling" with the familiar block chords indicated by the chord designations F, Bb and C₇ (I, IV and V₇).

LITTLE DUCKLINGS

Heads are in the wa - ter, tails are in the air.
Now they're right side up, and now they're up - side down.

After you are comfortable with this chording, try the three broken chord patterns which have been notated under part of the melody.

etc.

Such broken chord patterns can be used for a number of songs. Transposed to the key of C, the quarter-note pattern would be suitable for "Love Somebody" (p. 1), "Billy Boy" (p. 28), and "Grandma Grunts" (p. 38). The eighth-note patterns could be used for "Go Tell Aunt Rhody" (p. 3) and "Lightly Row" (p. 5).

Similar patterns can also be used in other meters. For songs in $\frac{4}{4}$ meter the chording could be one of the following:

Use these patterns, with the indicated chord changes, for your accompaniment to "Long, Long Ago."

LONG, LONG AGO

Andante

Thomas H. Bayly

Tell me the tales that to me were so dear, Long, long a-go,

Long, long a-go, Sing me the songs I de-light-ed to hear,

Long, long a-go long a-go. Now you are come all my

grief is re-moved, Let me for-get that so long I have roved

Let me be-lieve that you love as you loved Long, long a-go, long a-go.

In $\frac{3}{4}$ meter the accompaniment might be in one of the following patterns:

162

Try both of these patterns with "Oh, Where Has My Little Dog Gone?"

OH, WHERE HAS MY LITTLE DOG GONE?

Oh where, oh where has my lit - tle dog gone?

Oh where oh where can he be? _____

With his tail cut short and his ears cut long,

Oh where, oh where, can he be? _____

Transposed to the key of C, the same patterns would be suitable for "Du, Du, Liegst mir im Herzen" (p. 22) and "Lavender's Blue" (p. 81).

TWO-HANDED (RHYTHMIC) CHORDING

Another type of accompaniment that is very convenient and easy to learn is chording with both hands, leaving the melody to be sung or played on an instrument. The way this is done is to play the chord root on the accented beat(s) with the left hand and the triad of the same chord, or one of its inversions, on the unaccented beats with the right hand.

163

The advantage of this type of chording is that you do not need to be concerned about playing the melody. You do, however, need a functional knowledge of the triads and their inversions, and these should be reviewed at this time. See Chapter 3, page 62.

This kind of chording is sometimes called *rhythmic chording* and it is especially effective with many of our well-known American folk songs. The harmonizations of these songs are usually based on the I, IV, and V₇ chords, and "Old Smoky" is a very good example of this type of song. *Sing* the tune as you *chord* the accompaniment.

OLD SMOKY

2. A-courtin's a pleasure, a-flirtin's a grief,
   a false-hearted lover is worse than a thief.

3. A thief he will rob you, and take what you save,
   but a false-hearted lover will send you to your grave.

4. It's raining, its hailing, the moon gives no light,
   my horses can't travel this dark road tonight.

5. I'll go up to Old Smoky, the mountain so high,
   where wild birds and turtle doves can hear my sad cry.

The same patterns, transposed to the key of G, are also suitable for "Sing Your Way Home."

SING YOUR WAY HOME

Cheerfully

Source Unknown

Sing your way home at the close of the day,

Sing your way home, drive the shad-ows a way.

Smile ev-'ry mile, for wher-ev-er you roam it will bright-en your road,

it will light-en your load, if you sing your way home.

An accompaniment of this type gives a proper lilt to "My Home's in Montana." In the key of D the chords would be:

[1] The sign ⌢ over the notes in the next-to-the-last measure is called a *fermata* (hold), indicating that these tones should be prolonged.

MY HOME'S IN MONTANA

My home's in Mon - ta - na, I wear a ban - da - na,

My spurs are of sil - ver, My po - ny is gray;

When rid - ing the rang - es, My luck nev - er chang - es,

With foot in the stir - rup I gal - lop a - way.

"Go In and Out the Window" is in $\frac{2}{4}$ meter and the chording pattern for this song could be one of these:

GO IN AND OUT THE WINDOW

Go in and out the win-dow, Go in and out the win-dow,

Go in and out the win-dow, As we have done be - fore.

2. Go forth and choose a partner (three times)
   As we have done before.

166

Which inversion of the right-hand triad and seventh chord did you prefer? Why?

These chording patterns might be used for "Shoo, Fly, Don't Bother Me" (p. 75) and "Merrily We Roll Along" (p. 78); transposed to the key of C they could be used for "Jingle at the Window" (p. 32) and "Short'nin' Bread" (p. 32).

The same chords would be suitable for "Old Chisholm Trail" with the rhythmic pattern adjusted to the $\frac{4}{4}$ meter:

OLD CHISHOLM TRAIL

Lively

Cowboy Song

Oh, come a-long, boys, and lis-ten to my tale,

I'll tell you all my trou-bles on the old Chis-holm trail,

Come a ti yi yip-py yip-py yay yip-py yay,

Come a ti yi yip-py yip-py yay.

Transposed to the key of C, the same chording patterns could be used for "Hey Lidee" (p. 40) and "Li'l 'Liza Jane" (p. 42). Transposed to the key of G, they would go well with "Polly Wolly Doodle" (p. 74).

When a chord continues for a number of beats or measures, an easy way to avoid monotony is to use the fifth of the chord in the bass alternating with the root:

Try this pattern with "Camptown Races."

CAMPTOWN RACES

Spiritedly

Stephen Foster

1. The Camp-town la-dies sing this song, Doo-dah, doo-dah!
   See those hor-ses round the bend, Doo-dah, doo-dah!

The Camp-town race track five miles long, Oh, doo-dah-day.
Guess that race will nev-er end, Oh, doo-dah-day.

Go'ing to run all night, Go'ing to run all day.

The— horse I fan-cy is the bob-tail nag; He'll walk a-way from the bay.

2. The long-tailed filly and the big black horse, Doodah, doodah!
   They fly the track and they both cut 'cross, Oh, doodahday.
   The blind horse stuck in a big mud hole, Doodah, doodah!
   Can't touch bottom with a ten foot pole, Oh Doodahday!

3. Old muley cow came on the track, Doodah, doodah!
   The bob-tail flung her over his back, Oh, doodahday.
   Then fly along like a railroad car, Doodah, doodah!
   Running a race with a shooting star, Oh, doodahday!

This type of accompaniment would be very appropriate for "Old Texas" (p. 104) and "Skip to My Lou" (p. 103). It can be very effective in minor keys as well. "Nobody Home" is in G minor and the chording pattern might be this:

Experiment with different inversions of the triad and seventh chord and find the ones which sound best to you.

NOBODY HOME

The following chording pattern may be played in the left hand alone as an accompaniment to the melody in the right hand. It may also be played with both hands, with the left hand playing the chord root and the right hand playing the broken chords, as an accompaniment for singing. Either way, it can lend an expressive character to songs like "Aloha Oe."

ALOHA OE

CHORDS FOR ACCOMPANIMENTS

10

Harmonizing Songs

Your experiences in music will eventually lead you to songs for which no chord designations are provided, and you will want to be able to determine how to select the proper chords for the accompaniment to such songs.

CHOOSING CHORDS FOR SONGS

If you examine the chords used to accompany songs in major and minor keys in the previous chapters, you will discover the following general principles of melody harmonization:

1. The first and last chords in the song are nearly always the I chord. The next to the last chord is usually the V_7 chord and sometimes the IV chord.

2. The melody notes most often harmonized are those which occur on the accented beat or beats.[1]

3. The melody note which is sounded with the chord is usually present in the selected chord.[2] If more than one chord is available for this note, choose the one most satisfactory to the ear.

4. Like phrases of the melody are usually harmonized with the same chords.

[1] In some songs it may be desirable to harmonize melody notes on other beats of the measure. See "Sing Your Way Home" (p. 165), "The Erie Canal" (p. 150), "Welsh Fishers' Song" (p. 144), and "Charlie Is My Darling" (p. 146).
[2] Occasionally a chord will be played on a melody note which is foreign to the chord. See last measure of "Billy Boy" (p. 28), "A Cradle Hymn" (p. 30), and "Grandma Grunts" (p. 38).

PROCEDURE FOR HARMONIZING SONGS

Whenever you find songs for which the chords are not designated, you can use the following procedure for harmonizing them:

1. Determine the key of the song from the key signature and the final note of the melody.

2. Make a chart of the chords which might be used in this key and of the notes contained in these chords.

   Example: Key of G major

   I or G chord: G-B-D
   IV or C chord: C-E-G
   V_7 or D_7 chord: D-F#-A-C

3. Decide which beat or beats of the measure you might like to chord.

   Examples: Songs in $\frac{2}{4}$, $\frac{3}{4}$, and $\frac{3}{8}$ meter are usually harmonized on the first beat of the measure.

   Songs in $\frac{4}{4}$ and $\frac{6}{8}$ meter are usually harmonized on the primary and secondary accents of each measure.

4. Choose a chord containing the melody note which is being harmonized and write the letter name and Roman numeral for this chord above and below, respectively, the melody note. (Sometimes a measure may contain several melody notes belonging to this chord.) You already know that the first and last chords of a song are likely to be the tonic chord (I).

5. If a melody note can be harmonized with more than one chord, write in the letter names and Roman numerals for these also; then choose the chord which sounds best to the ear when played in context with the preceding and following chords.

6. Look for like phrases in the song and use the same harmonization for these.

Analyze the chords which have been written out for "Twinkle, Twinkle, Little Star" with reference to the above six points. Check measures 3, 5, and 7 for possible choices of chords. What might these be? Are you satisfied with the chords chosen?

TWINKLE, TWINKLE LITTLE STAR

French Folk Song

Nonharmonic Tones. All the tones in the melody of "Twinkle, Twinkle, Little Star" were present in the chords used for its harmonization. However, every tone of a melody does not have to be a chord tone and melody tones which are not chord tones are called *nonharmonic tones*. The melody to "London Bridge" exemplifies two kinds of nonharmonic tones: *neighboring tones* (*) and *passing tones* (+). A neighboring tone moves step-wise (up or down) from a chord tone and returns to the *same* tone. A passing tone moves step-wise between two *different* chord tones.

LONDON BRIDGE

There are no absolute rules of right and wrong to guide you in the harmonization of songs; any given melody may be harmonized in several ways depending on the extent of your knowledge of chords and on your musical discrimination. For the time being, your knowledge of chords is presumably limited to the chords you have been using thus far for songs in major and minor keys. But with these at your disposal, you can make up satisfactory accompaniments to many songs. Test your understanding of the procedure we have suggested for harmonizing songs by making up accompaniments for "Old Folks at Home" and "Green Grow the Lilacs."

OLD FOLKS AT HOME

GREEN GROW THE LILACS

With feeling

American Folk Song

Oh green grow the li - lacs and soft falls the dew

How sad's been the day since I part - ed from you,

But at our next meet - ing, our love we'll re - new

We'll change the green li - lac for the Red, White and Blue.

THE SUPERTONIC CHORD

Occasionally you will encounter songs in which the II chord or *supertonic chord* can be used very effectively for a more satisfactory harmonization.

The II chord may be used to harmonize scale tones 2 and 4 in place of the V_7 chord, as in "Oh, Dear, What Can the Matter Be?" Here you will find it alternating with the V_7 chord in the seventh measure of the refrain and in the third, fourth, and seventh measures of the verse. This interchange of chords adds variety and interest to the harmonization. Play the accompaniment first with the chords indicated and then try it with the G_7 chord as a substitute for the Dm chord. Which do you prefer?

OH, DEAR! WHAT CAN THE MATTER BE?

Gaily

English Folk Song

REFRAIN

Oh, dear! What can the mat-ter be? Dear, dear, what can the mat-ter be?

Oh, dear! What can the mat-ter be? John-ny's so long at the fair.____

VERSE

1. He prom-ised to buy me a trin-ket to please me, And then, for a smile, Oh,
2. He prom-ised to bring me a bas-ket of po-sies, A gar-land of lil-ies,

he vowed he would tease me, He prom-ised to bring me a bunch of blue rib-bons
A gift of red ros-es, A lit-tle straw hat to set off the blue rib-bons

To tie up my bon-ny brown hair.____
That tie up my bon-ny brown hair.____

The supertonic chord is frequently used with the third of the chord raised a half step (#3) thus making it a major chord instead of a minor chord as it would be ordinarily. This chord may be used as a triad, II#3 (or II#), or it may be used as a seventh chord, II$\frac{\#3}{7}$ (or II$\frac{\#}{7}$), the 7 being the usual designation for a seventh chord.

C major

Note the use of this chord (D₇), in "In the Good Old Summer Time."

IN THE GOOD OLD SUMMERTIME

Ron Shields

Waltz time

George Evans

In the good old sum - mer time,_____

in the good old sum - mer time,_____

Stroll - ing through the sha - dy lanes,

with your ba - by mine;_____

You hold her hand and she holds yours,

and that's a ve - ry good sign,_____

That she's your toot - sy woot - sy in the

good old sum - mer time._____

178

The II $\frac{\#}{7}$ chord is also used very effectively in this harmonization of "All Through the Night."

ALL THROUGH THE NIGHT

Andante   Welsh Folk Song

1. Sleep, my child, and peace at-tend thee, All through the night;
2. While the moon her watch is keep-ing, All through the night;

Guard-ian an-gels God will send thee, All through the night.
While the wea-ry world is sleep-ing, All through the night.

Soft the drow-sy hours are creep-ing, Hill and vale in slum-ber steep-ing,
O'er thy spir-it gen-tly steal-ing Vi-sions of de-light re-veal-ing,

I my lov-ing vig-il keep-ing, All through the night.
Breathes a pure and ho-ly feel-ing, All through the night.

THE MEDIANT AND SUBMEDIANT CHORDS

Two chords which may help you in harmonizing somewhat complex melodies are the *mediant chord* (III) built on the third degree of the scale and the *submediant chord* (VI) built on the sixth scale degree.[3]

G major   1   2   3   4   5   6   7   8

[3] On the Autoharp these chords are available only in C and F major and in A and D minor.

You have already encountered the III chord in the accompaniments to "When Johnny Comes Marching Home" (p. 147) and "Charlie Is My Darling" (p. 146). Review these songs at this time.

"The First Noel" provides an opportunity to use the VI chord very effectively. Using a chord on the first and third beat of each measure, you may harmonize it in this manner:

THE FIRST NOEL

The harmonization of "The Canadian" utilizes both the II and VI chords in addition to other familiar chords.

THE CANADIAN

Yvonne Carr

Smoothly

French-Canadian Folk Tune

1. Down where the riv - er flows, Where the tall pine tree grows,
2. "Riv - er, if you should see Those who are dear to me,

I met a lad one day. Sad - ly I heard him say,
Tell them you know my tears. For all the by - gone years.

"Wea - ry of paths I roam, Lone - ly am I for home,
And tho' I'm far a - way, I will re - turn to stay,

Long - ing to find my friends, Where the Saint Law - rence bends."
Nev - er to say good-bye, To the Ca - na - dian sky."

Reprinted from H. R. Wilson *et al.*, *Growing With Music*, Book 5 (Englewood Cliffs, N.J.: Prentice-Hall, Inc., 1966), p. 24, by permission of the publisher.

We shall conclude our discussion of harmonizing songs with a very beautiful song, "Tell Me Why." The harmonization of this melody utilizes another new chord, the *diminished seventh chord* (VII°) (see p. 61), as well as nearly every chord that you have learned to use previously. The variety of chords needed for the accompaniment precludes the use of the Autoharp for this purpose, but we are sure that you will have little difficulty in playing this song on the piano in this arrangement.

TELL ME WHY

182

11

Composing Songs

Creative music activities in the classroom may take many forms and the composing of songs can be a motivating and highly satisfying musical experience. Furthermore, when one creates and notates his own songs, he demonstrates his ability to utilize musical knowledge. To this extent writing songs can also provide a functional review of many of the music fundamentals learned through singing, playing, and analyzing music.

CREATING A SONG

Among the approaches to creative song writing used in the elementary school are (1) choosing a poem which appeals to the imagination and giving it a musical setting and (2) writing an original poem and composing a suitable melody for it.

Basically there are four problems involved in composing a song:

1. Determining the rhythm and the meter of the words of the poem.

2. Translating the word-rhythm into line-notation.

3. Devising a melody which will express the meaning of the words or mood of the poem.

4. Notating the melody on the staff in a suitable key for singing.

Let us look into a fourth-grade classroom to see what is being done with this type of musical activity. One of the students has made up the following little jingle:

"The human body is such a funny thing;
It has so many organs but they don't play a thing!"

The class enjoys these words and reads them in unison several times until everyone agrees that they are in the following rhythm:

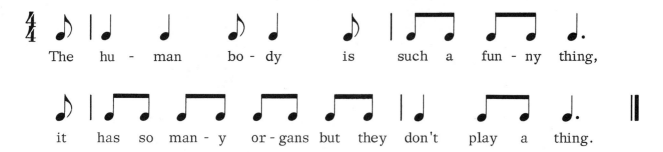

After establishing the rhythm of the words and translating that rhythm into note-values, all that remains is to put a tune to the words. Because this is a short verse, these fourth-graders, experienced in creating melodies, have little difficulty in deciding upon the following melody:

4	The	hu - man bo - dy is	such a fun - ny thing,
4	5	8 8 5 5 5	6 6 6 6 5

it	has so man - y or - gans but they	don't play a thing.
5	6 6 6 6 5 5 4 4	3 2 2 1

The teacher, who already has the words written on the chalkboard beneath the treble staff, has the task of deciding in which key to write this tune. Because the range of the melody is within one octave, she chooses the key of **D** major. This key places the song in a good singing range for the class. The song looked like this when it was completed:

THE HUMAN BODY

The children then copied the song into their notebooks so that they might have a permanent record of it for singing or playing at home or at some later time in school.

THE RHYTHM OF WORDS IN NOTATION

These children demonstrated that the first step in notating a song is to discover the rhythm and meter of the words. The procedure for this was to read the poem aloud as a rhythmic chant and to notate this in line-notation (see Chapter 1, p. 3) with barlines inserted to the left of the most heavily accented words or word-syllables.

The hu - man bod -y is | such a fun- ny thing
it | has so man -y or-gans but they | don't play a thing!

Deciding on the proper meter for the rhyme posed a problem because the meter of this jingle could be either duple or quadruple; however, the word-rhythm of the second line with the emphasis on the word "don't" seemed to indicate the latter.

The line-notation was then translated into music notation with the quarter note as the beat unit shown above. Notice that the children sensed that this poem would call for a "pick-up" note at the beginning (♪) and that the note values of the last measure would have to "complement" this note to make up a full measure (♩♩ ♩ ♩♩.). Notice also that they placed the most important words or word-syllables on the accented beats and the less important words, such as "the," "it," and "a," on the unaccented beats.

Word Rhythms in Common Meters. In preparing to notate your own songs you may need practice in translating the rhythm of words into notation. The cheers used at athletic events are sometimes excellent word-rhythms to notate. Perhaps the best known of these is "We want a touchdown!" First we write the words, then:

1. Speak the words (to find line notation and accents).

We want a touch-down! We want a
— — — — — — — —

2. Place bar lines left of heavily accented words.

— — —|— —|— — —

3. Translate into music notation.

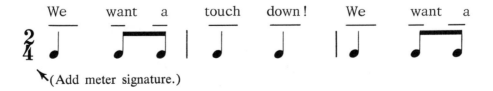

We   want a   touch down! We   want a

²/₄

↖(Add meter signature.)

185

Following the above example, continue with the following words we have selected to help you translate word rhythms into notation. The first two are in duple or quadruple meter, $\frac{2}{4}$ or $\frac{4}{4}$. After you have worked with the first two examples, look at their notation in the book to be sure you are proceeding correctly.

1. Are you sleep-ing, are you sleep-ing, broth-er John? — broth-er John? (p. 100).

2. Go tell Aunt Rho-dy the old gray goose is dead. (p. 3)

3. Ding dong bell, — Pus-sy's in the well. —

4. Peas por-ridge hot; peas por-ridge cold,
   Peas por-ridge in the pot, nine days old. —

5. Baa baa black sheep, have you an-y wool? —
   Yes sir, yes sir, three bags full. —

A helpful hint is that unimportant words such as "a" and "the" are very rarely on accented beats of the mesaure. They are also ordinarily assigned to notes of relatively short duration. Important words are almost always on accented beats and have notes of longer value.

Next try to notate words in $\frac{3}{4}$ or $\frac{3}{8}$ meter. The first two examples are from songs in this book. First notate the word rhythms; then compare what you have written with the notation in the book.

1. Du, Du, liegst mir in Herzen (p. 22)

2. Sing your way home at the close of the day (p. 165)

3. Sweetly I sing to you under the moon

4. We wish you a merry Christmas, we wish you a merry Christmas

The following words should be notated in fast $\frac{6}{8}$ meter. Starting with the words you know in the first example will help you to identify the characteristic rhythmic patterns in this meter: , and
 .

1. Lit-tle Tom Tin-ker got burned with a clink-er and
   He be-gan to cry —
   "Ma-a, Ma-a, what a poor fel-low am I." (p. 98)

2. Lit-tle Boy Blue, come blow your horn, — the
   Sheep's in the mead-ow, the cow's in the corn.

3. He's a jol-ly good fel-low, which no-bod-y can deny. —

Sometimes it is difficult to decide which meter signature to use when the rhythm of the words can be expressed equally well in either of two meters. An example of this is "Row, Row, Row Your Boat," which frequently appears in this rhythmic notation:

STEPS IN COMPOSING SONGS

Now try to create and notate some songs of your own. This can be done by you alone or as a cooperative project by the class as described below. The best poems to begin with are those in which the words have a simple and direct rhythm such as:

FOG

The fog is rising slowly
Soon it will be high;
Then the gulls will soar again
Far up in the sky.

1. Write the words under the treble staff on the chalkboard or in a notebook. Discuss the meaning and mood of the poem and look for words which could suggest the rise or fall of the melody line.

2. Speak the words in unison until everyone feels the same word-rhythm. Your class might feel the rhythm of this poem to be either $\frac{2}{4}$ or $\frac{6}{8}$ meter.

3. Find and mark the most heavily accented words. (Clapping the word-rhythm and conducting the meter can help in steps 2 and 3.)

4. Place barlines in front of the most heavily accented words or word-syllables. Remember that some poems require a "pick-up" note before the first barline.

5. Find a melody for the first line. This can be done in several different ways.

The class can first *think* the melody silently, then sing it aloud, and accept the majority opinion. Or several individuals can contribute their different melodies, and the class will decide which of them is best suited to the mood and thought of the words. Some class members might choose the Song Bells, piano, or other instruments as the medium by which they create their melodies.

6. Sing the chosen melody several times until everyone in the class can remember it.

7. Write the numbers, syllables, or letter names of the melody under the words.

8. Continue this process with the second line of the words. One way to do this is to sing the first line, then silently think the melody of the second line. Then repeat this; only this time, sing the second line. Then choose the best melody, sing it several times (from the beginning of the song) to established it firmly in everyone's mind, and write the numbers or syllable names beneath the words.

9. Continue in the above manner to the end of the poem.

10. Translate the numbers or syllable names into notation. First, select the key you will use by placing the song in the best singing range according to its highest and lowest tones. Next, place the notes on the staff.

11. Harmonize the melody on piano or Autoharp in accordance with the principles of harmonization which you learned in Chapter 6.

12. Make appropriate use of the tempo and expression marks you have learned in previous chapters of this book.

With experience in this activity you will learn to write music that reflects the mood of the words and to ask questions and answer questions with your melody and your harmony. You may also wish to add chants and descants to some of your songs.

Try setting some of the following poems to music.

> Gather ye rosebuds while ye may,
> Old Time is still a-flying;
> And this same flow'r that smiles today,
> Tomorrow will be dying.
>
> *Robert Herrick (1591-1674)*

> I met a little cottage girl:
> She was eight years old, she said;
> Her hair was thick with many a curl
> That clustered 'round her head.
>
> *William Wordsworth (1770-1850)*

> Books! 'tis a dull and endless strife:
> Come, hear the woodland linnet,
> How sweet his music! on my life
> There's more of wisdom in it.
>
> *William Wordsworth (1770-1850)*

> There she weaves by night and day
> A magic web with colors gay.
> She has heard a whisper say

A curse is on her if she stay
To look down to Camelot.

Alfred, Lord Tennyson (1809-1892)

Ring out the old, ring in the new,
Ring, happy bells, across the snow:
The year is going, let him go;
Ring out the false, ring in the true.

Alfred, Lord Tennyson (1809-1892)

WINTER

Snow is falling silently,
The wind is standing still.
Birds are making little tracks
Upon the window sill.

MOONLIGHT

Dark is the night as I lie in my bed;
The stars and the moon give light.
As I lie in my bed, resting my head,
I go to sleep; I go to sleep.

THE SNOWMAN

I wish I were a snowman,
So fat and round and still;
Then I would watch the children,
Come sliding down the hill.

DEVELOPING SKILLS

1. Notate some of your favorite cheers used at athletic events.

2. Word-rhythms played on a drum have been called "drum-talk." Play on a drum, then notate geographical names such as Mississippi River; Portland, Oregon; and Birmingham, Alabama.

3. Compare "A Cradle Hymn" (p. 30) and "Cradle Song" (p. 77) to find out if you can explain why the first song is in $\frac{4}{4}$ meter while the second one is in $\frac{2}{4}$ meter.

4. Choose some nursery rhymes and poems from other sources and set them to music.

5. Create your own poems and set them to music. (It is not always necessary for words to rhyme.)

6. Harmonize your songs, choosing a type of accompaniment suited to the mood of the poem.

7. Try to write down the original songs of classmates as they sing them. This will take practice.

12

Concepts of Musical Form

All works of art have form of some kind. Form in music is the way in which rhythm, melody, and harmony are put together to make a unified whole. You have already become familiar with some of the basic concepts of musical form: melodic movement and contour, phrases and cadences, rhythmic and melodic motives, repetition and sequence, two- and three-part forms. In this chapter we shall examine the formal aspects of music more fully and also extend our knowledge of musical form to include some of the larger forms of music through recorded examples of instrumental music.

PHRASE AND CADENCE

The phrase may be considered the basic unit of musical structure. It usually contains one or more melodic or rhythmic motives used in repetition or sequence. Cadences are musical punctuation marks or phrase endings. They may be conclusive (complete) or inconclusive (incomplete); the degree of finality is dependent upon rhythmic, melodic, or harmonic movement.

From a rhythmic standpoint, cadences usually occur on a note of long duration or on a relatively long note followed by a rest. Melodically, a cadence is considered complete when the phrase ends on the tonic and incomplete when it ends on any other tone. Harmonically, cadences are defined in terms of the chord progression which occurs at the end of the phrases. They are classified as follows:

Half cadence: phrase ending on V or V$_7$.

Authentic cadence: phrase ending on I preceded by V or V$_7$.

Plagal cadence: phrase ending on I preceded by IV.

Deceptive cadence: phrase ending on unexpected chord.

Phrase lengths of two, four, or eight measures may be considered the norm. However, phrases may vary greatly in length and in clarity, and it is not always easy to determine where one phrase ends and another begins.

PERIOD AND PHRASE GROUP

The period, sometimes called *sentence*, consists of two phrases with contrasting cadences. The first phrase, the *antecedent*, is usually terminated by a half cadence; the second, or *consequent* phrase, terminates with an authentic cadence. The period is said to be a complete musical statement.

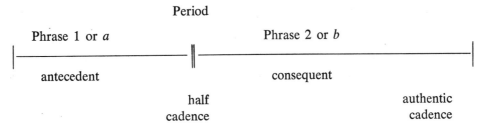

The *double period* consists of four phrases with a half cadence in the middle and an authentic cadence at the end.

The *phrase group* is a unit of three or more phrases, sometimes of unequal length, the last of which ends with an authentic cadence.

The following songs exemplify the above phrase forms. Analyze the cadences to reinforce your understanding of these concepts.

Period

"Love Somebody"	p. 1
"He's Got the Whole World in His Hands"	p. 41
"Four in a Boat"	p. 83

Double Period

"Billy Boy"	p. 28
"Lavender's Blue"	p. 81
"When the Saints Go Marching In"	p. 86

Phrase Group

"Oh, No, John"	p. 84
"Three Blind Mice"	p. 102
"Sing Your Way Home"	p. 165

SONG FORMS

In Chapter 1 the phrase structure of songs was examined and it was discovered that phrases may repeat exactly, that they may repeat with some variation, or that they may be different and thus contrasting. Phrases were found to be arranged in ways which resulted in two-part (*binary*) and three-part (*ternary*) song forms. Songs consisting of either a single phrase or a repeated phrase constitute a one-part (*unitary*) song form. However, the song forms tend to outgrow the simple phrase arrangement in more complex songs and in instrumental compositions. These may have a period, a double period, or a phrase group as one of the parts of the song form. Thus, the concept of what constitutes a particular song form must include a consideration of these possibilities. When analyzing the longer forms it is customary to designate the separate phrases by small letters (a, b, c, d, etc.) and to label the various parts with capital letters (A, AB, ABA). The following songs are representative of the three song forms. Analyze the songs by observing the cadences and indicate the phrase arrangement in the space provided.

		Page	Phrase Arrangement
One-Part Song Form (A)	"Whistle, Daughter, Whistle"	6	_____
	"Deaf Woman's Courtship"	2	_____
	"A Cradle Hymn"	30	_____
Two-Part Song Form (AB)	"Go Tell Aunt Rhody"	3	_____
	"Du, Du, Liegst Mir im Herzen"	22	_____
	"Li'l 'Liza Jane"	42	_____
Three-Part Song Form (ABA)	"Lightly Row"	5	_____
	"Rosa, Come and Go Dancing"	35	_____
	"Cradle Song"	36	_____
	"Shoo, Fly, Don't Bother Me"	75	_____

The immediate repetition of a phrase or a section is not considered to add another part to the form. Furthermore, musical forms are not precise "set" forms but are instead generalized concepts which permit different arrangements or orders of phrases or sections. Larger musical forms are subject to even more variation in structure.

Binary and ternary forms are also encountered frequently in instrumental music. In some instances they will be very simple in structure, but at other times they may be more varied and complex. The following recorded examples illustrate different arrangements of binary and ternary structures.[1]

MINUET FROM "DON GIOVANNI"

Mozart
MSB 78003

[1] The recorded instrumental compositions referred to in this book may be found in the following Educational Record Series:

Adventures in Music (RCA–Victor)—AIM

Bowmar Orchestral Library (Bowmar Records)—BOL

Musical Sound Books (The Sound Book Press Society)—MSB

MINUET IN G

The binary form played an important role in the music written in the Baroque period (see Chapter 13). It was a highly stylized form and the material of the two parts, A and B, was closely related. The first part would modulate to a related key, closing with a cadence in this key. The second part would begin in the new key, then modulate back to the original (tonic) key. The B section would frequently be made up of material taken from the A section through simple repetition or a kind of development. It is often somewhat longer than the A section.

BADINERIE FROM SUITE NO. 2
IN B MINOR FOR FLUTE AND STRINGS

Additional examples of binary form:

Ginastera: "Wheat Dance" from *Estansia*	AIM	IV-1
Handel: Bourée and Menuetto from *Royal Fireworks Music*	AIM	III-2
	BOL	62
Milhaud: "Copacabana" from *Saudades do Brazil*	AIM	IV-2
Respighi: "Danza" from *Brazilian Impressions*	AIM	V-2

The basic scheme of the ternary form is *statement-departure-restatement* (ABA), but this may be enlarged and expanded by repetition of sections, introductions, interludes, and codas. The key to listening is to recognize the return of the first section (A).

BALLET OF THE SYLPHS
FROM "DAMNATION OF FAUST"

Berlioz
AIM I

TREPAK FROM "NUTCRACKER SUITE"

Tchaikovsky
BOL 58

Additional examples of ternary form:

Brahms: Hungarian Dance No. 1 in C Minor   AIM   V-2
Copland: Circus Music   AIM   III-1
Debussy: *En Bateau*   BOL   53
Offenbach: Barcarolle from *Tales of Hoffman*   AIM   III-1
Schumann: *Traumerei*   AIM   IV-2
    BOL   63
Stravinsky: Berceuse from *Firebird Suite*   AIM   I
Vaughan-Williams: Fantasia on "Greensleeves"   AIM   VI-2
Walton: Waltz from *Façade* Suite   AIM   VI-2

The *compound ternary* form is an extended structure in which each part may be a simple binary or ternary form in itself. This form is used consistently in the classical minuets of Haydn and Mozart. The middle part (B) is called *Trio* while the outer parts are called *Minuet*. This form may be diagramed as follows:

194

Note that when the minuet is restated, the two parts, A and B, are not repeated.

MENUETTO FROM SYMPHONY NO.6 IN G MAJOR

Haydn
BOL 63

Additional examples of compound ternary form:

Bizet: Minuetto from *L'Arlessienne* Suite No. 1	AIM	IV-2
Mozart: Menuetto from Divertimento No. 17 in D	AIM	V-2
Mozart: Minuet from Symphony No. 40 in G Minor	BOL	62
Sousa: March, "Stars and Stripes Forever"	AIM	IV-2
	BOL	60

RONDO FORM

The structural plan of the rondo is the alternation of a *principal* theme with one or more *subordinate* themes. The principal theme must occur at least three times. These restatements may be in the form of exact repetitions, or variants, or abbreviations. The subordinate themes present new materials and new key centers. Themes may vary in length from a single phrase to one of the song forms.

The rondo design may be expressed in formulas such as ABACA, ABACADA, and so on. As can be seen, the recurrence of "A" is the unique characteristic of the rondo form. The exact number of divisions in a rondo is not prescribed and the order of repetition of themes is frequently varied. Furthermore, the themes may be separated by *episodes* or *transitions* made up of nonthematic materials. A *coda* based upon the principal theme may terminate the piece.

GAVOTTE (AMARYLLIS)

Additional examples of rondo form:

Beethoven: Scherzo from Symphony No. 7 in A Major	BOL	62
Dvorak: Slavonic Dance in C Minor	AIM	IV-2
Haydn: Gypsy Rondo from Trio in G Major	BOL	64
Khachaturian: Waltz from *Masquerade* Suite	AIM	IV-2
Mozart: Romanza from *Eine Kleine Nachtmusik*	AIM	IV-1
	MSB	78004
Prokofieff: "Waltz on Ice" from *Winter Holiday*	AIM	III-2
Smetana: "Dance of the Comedians" from *Bartered Bride*	AIM	VI-2
	BOL	56
Tchaikowsky: Waltz from *Sleeping Beauty*	AIM	IV-1

VARIATION FORM

Variation is both a device and a form. As a device, it may be applied to any musical element—rhythm, melody, or harmony—in any of the musical forms. As a form, variation refers to a piece of music which is structured entirely upon the application of variation techniques.

There are two categories of variation forms: *sectional variations* in which the individual variations are separated from one another and *continuous variations* in which each new variation merges with the preceding one without any noticeable interruption.

The design of the sectional variation form, known as *theme and variations*, involves the statement of a theme followed by a number of restatements—the variations. The theme is usually in binary or ternary form. The variations retain the basic form of the theme while alterations occur in the melody, rhythm, or harmony; changes in tonality and tempo may also occur.

196

Theme

Haydn

BOL 62

Continuous variations are known as *ground, ground bass* or *basso ostinato, passacaglia,* and *chaconne*. In the ground a short melodic motive is repeated over and over again in the bass while the upper voices proceed in normal fashion. In the passacaglia the ground bass motive becomes a melody of several measures and it may be transferred to other voices in the texture. The chaconne is very similar to the passacaglia, the main difference being that the theme is based upon a series of chords rather than a melodic line. However, the distinction between these two forms is more theoretical than practical as far as the listener is concerned.

A GROUND

Handel
BOL 53

PASSACAGLIA IN C MINOR

Bach
Standard Recording

Additional examples of variation form:

Anderson: "The Girl I Left Behind Me"	AIM	V-2
Caillet: Variations on "Pop! Goes the Weasel"	AIM	IV-1
	BOL	65
Copland: "Simple Gifts" from *Appalachian Spring*	BOL	65
	MSB	78152
Guarnieri: Brazilian Dance	AIM	VI-2
	BOL	55

SONATA FORM

A *sonata* is a multi-movement work for one or two instruments. It usually contains three or four contrasting pieces of large design. A *symphony* is a sonata for orchestra; a *quartet* is a sonata for four instruments; a *quintet* is a sonata for five instruments; a *concerto* is a sonata for a solo instrument and orchestra.

The term *sonata form*, or *sonata-allegro form*, refers to the structural design utilized most frequently in the first movement of sonatas of the above types. It is a large three-part form consisting of *exposition* (A)–*development* (B)–*recapitulation* (A).

In the exposition the thematic material of the movement is presented. This consists of a *principal theme* and a *subordinate theme* and these themes will often be in one of the smaller song forms. The principal theme is usually vigorous and dramatic in character and is always in the tonic key of the movement. The subordinate theme is generally more lyrical in character and is stated in the dominant key. The exposition may also include a *closing theme* (*codetta*) and *bridge passages* (*transitions*) between the principal and subordinate themes and between the subordinate and closing themes.

The development section is devoted to a "working out" of the materials presented in the exposition. This may take the form of presenting fragments of the themes (*motives*) in various combinations and in several keys. The motives may be altered melodically and rhythmically and may be combined in new contexts and into contrapuntal texture. Frequently, only one of the themes may be utilized in this manner, as in the Schubert example below. At the end of the development section there will usually be a *retransition* passage, the purpose of which is to re-establish the tonic key in which the recapitulation occurs.

The recapitulation section is essentially a repetition of the exposition. However, in this section the subordinate (and closing theme, if any) must now appear in the tonic key.

Two additional sections are often included in the sonata form, namely an *introduction* and a *coda*. The introduction is usually slow in tempo and only rarely contains reference to materials presented in the exposition. The coda, on the other hand, is quite often based on thematic material; new material may also be introduced, in which case the coda may become quite lengthy.

The sonata-allegro form may be outlined as follows:

Introduction
(optional)

A   *Exposition*
{ Principal theme in tonic key
Bridge passage (transition)
Subordinate theme in dominant key
Codetta or closing theme

B   *Development*
{ "Working out" of thematic material
Retransition to tonic key

A   *Recapitulation*
{ Principal theme in tonic key
Bridge passage (transition)
Subordinate theme in tonic key
Coda or concluding theme in tonic key

The Schubert example used to illustrate the sonata-allegro form contains the following: (1) a very brief introduction, (2) presentation of principal and subordinate themes (each repeated) both followed by related transition passages, (3) short development on a motive from the principal theme, (4) recapitulation of the two themes with related transitional passages, and (5) a short coda.

SYMPHONY NO. 5 IN B FLAT
(FIRST MOVEMENT)

Schubert
AIM V-1

Principal Theme
Allegro

Subordinate Theme

Additional examples of sonata-allegro form:

Prokofieff: Classical Symphony   MSB   78102-3
Zador: Children's Symphony   BOL   64

CONTRAPUNTAL OR POLYPHONIC FORMS

The terms contrapuntal and polyphonic are often used synonymously with reference to music which contains two or more rhythmically and melodically distinctive parts or "voices." The combining of such parts is called counterpoint ("point against point"). Polyphonic compositions are usually classified in terms of the contrapuntal techniques which the composer employs in the composition of a musical work and they seldom conform to any set pattern of design. The overall form of a particular composition is always dependent on the musical content rather than on a formalized design. Nevertheless, musicians tend to use the term *form* in discussing contrapuntal music and the most familiar polyphonic forms are the *canon* and the *fugue*.

Canon. A canon is a form in which a melody is imitated strictly by one or more voices after a given time and at a particular interval. The familiar *round* is a type of canon which is always sung or played in unison or octaves by two or more individuals. As a form the canon is not suitable for extended compositions. However, it is frequently employed by composers in brief compositions or in sections of larger compositions. When so used, it is referred to as *canonic imitation*. The Farandole by Bizet listed below is a good example of the use of this contrapuntal technique.

Fugue. The fugue is a polyphonic composition of two or more voices or instruments which develops a short melodic theme, called a *subject,* through contrapuntal means. A good fugue subject will contain one or more characteristic motives that are readily recognizable.

All fugues begin with an *exposition*. Structurally, this is the most rigid section of this form. Using a four-voiced fugue as an example the exposition would consist of the following:

1. The presentation of the fugue subject alone in one voice in the tonic key.

2. The imitation (*answer*) of this subject in the dominant key, a fifth above or a fourth below.

3. The presentation of a new subject (*counter-subject*) as a continuation of the fugue subject and heard simultaneously with the answer.

4. The restatement of the fugue subject in the tonic key, one octave below the first statement.

5. The answer to this restatement while it continues with the counter-subject.

6. The concluding cadence which is usually on the dominant if the fugue is in a major key or on the tonic of the relative major if it is in a minor key.

After the first subject and answer there may be a short transitional passage, *episode,* used for the purpose of modulating into the proper key for the restatement. Also, after the subject and countersubject have been exposed in any one voice, this voice is free to continue in an unrestricted manner as a *free voice.*

200

The exposition of a four-voiced fugue may be diagrammed thus:

Soprano S———— CS_ _ _ FV . . . . .

Alto   S———— CS_ _ _ (E) FV . . . . .

Tenor   S———— CS_ _ _ FV . . . .

Bass   S——— CS_ _ _ (E) Cadence

S—Subject, CS—Countersubject, E—Episode, FV—Free Voice

Following the exposition the structure of the fugue is usually free, consisting of alternating statements of the fugue subject and episodes in related keys. The episodes may be based on fragments of the subject or countersubject or upon new material. The fugue subject itself may be altered in different ways, shortened or lengthened, augmented, inverted, and so forth.

Toward the end of the fugue a *stretto* may appear. This is the name given to a passage in which the subject is imitated by another voice before it has been completely stated in the first voice. However, all fugues end with a clear and complete statement of the subject. The final cadence is sometimes preceded by or built upon a sustained tone, *pedal point,* held in the bass independently of the accompanying voices.

LITTLE FUGUE IN G MINOR

Bach
AIM VI-1

Additional examples of polyphonic compositions:

Bach: "Jesu, Joy of Man's Desiring" from Cantata No. 147	AIM	V-1
	BOL	62
	MSB	78316
McBride: Pumpkineater's Little Fugue	BOL	65
Bizet: Farandole from *L'Arlessienne* Suite No. 2	AIM	VI-1
Thomson: Fugue and Choral on "Yankee Doodle"	BOL	65

13

Style Periods in Music

Musical style is concerned with the manner and ways in which musical thought is expressed. In order to more fully understand musical styles, it is necessary to be familiar with the main historical periods. Throughout history, artistic expression has been influenced by political, social, and economic forces which have resulted in basic changes in styles. Because these changes are evolutionary some stylistic elements tend to overlap. For example, the years 1800 to 1820 reveal characteristics of both Classical style and early Romantic style. The listener reflects his knowledge of basic styles when he becomes able to respond to music in ways such as, "That sounds like the music of Bach," or "This is music which could have been written in no other time than in our own century." The most widely accepted approach to the study of style is in relation to periods.

The music of the Medieval and Renaissance periods is, perhaps, only of passing interest to the average layman. It was, however, during the twelfth, thirteenth, and fourteenth centuries that the development of many-voiced (*polyphonic*) music, as opposed to one-voiced (*monophonic*) music, took place as well as the movement from modal to tonal music. Composers of the twelfth and thirteenth centuries utilized triple meters and repeated rhythm patterns, while those of the fourteenth century preferred duple meter with less rigid rhythmic treatment. Vocal music predominated although instruments were used. The harmony sounds harsh and bleak to our ears. The music had a thin texture and it was modal. Music of the fifteenth and sixteenth centuries remained polyphonic, but major and minor tonalities grew in popularity among the still dominant modes. This music is easily identified as "not as old," and much of it is acceptable as beautiful music to our twentieth-century ears. Barlines were seldom used; the music was generally unmetered, that is, the meter signature was not used as it is today. Instead, the stress and rhythm of words governed rhythm and meter with a result that the music was generally smooth and flowing. The polyphony reflected the same basic harmonic concepts we understand today; the rhythm was more complex than that of the earlier music. Imitation was widely used. This is a composer's device in which a melodic idea is restated by another voice or voices in close succession. Palestrina is the best-known composer of this period. Nearly all composers wrote for the church as he did.

While this earlier music is of interest, music with which we are in contact today is usually of no earlier time than that of the Baroque period.

THE BAROQUE PERIOD (1600-1750)

The beginning of this important period was marked by the emergence of the solo song, apparently in an attempt to balance the emphasis on polyphony which continued throughout the period. These songs were accompanied by bass instruments and early keyboard instruments, notably the harpsichord, and this accompanying part had a *figured bass* (or *thorough-bass*) consisting of a written bass line with figures (numerals) which indicated the part the bass instruments were to play and the harmony which was thus directed to be improvised by the harpsichordist. The figured bass is a dominant characteristic of the period and was utilized in many types of music from opera to instrumental pieces. This style of music is called *homophonic*.

These were exciting times in which to live. Great names in science included Newton and Harvey, in literature there were Moliere and Milton, and in art Rubens and Rembrandt. It was an age of expansion, discovery, and exploration, and the arts reflected this with aspects of expansiveness, grandeur, and impressiveness. Opera was created as a new musical form and performed for the public on a lavish scale little known today. Other new forms included the oratorio, cantata, fugue, overture, trio sonata, concerto grosso, and chorale prelude. Instrumental music grew in popularity, but the orchestra was not yet standardized as we know it today, and all manner of instrumental combinations flourished. Sometimes vocalists and instrumentalists performed from the same score in more or less formal presentations. Dance music became music to be listened to as well as danced to; these dances included the sarabande, allemande, and gigue, and they were put together to form the instrumental suite. Among the instruments of that day were the viola de gamba, viola d'amore, lute, recorder, and high-pitched trumpets without valves, for the brass instrument valve was not invented until the nineteenth century.

The old modes were gradually abandoned in favor of the major and minor modes which are dominant in the periods to follow. Polyphony became firmly integrated into the system of major-minor tonality. Dynamics consisted mainly of loud or soft—the crescendo and decrescendo were not favored, possibly because of the inflexibility of many of the instruments—so we are likely to hear clear dynamic levels similar to terraces. The rhythm was steady, with a regular accent which was emphasized by the bass parts. This was the "new rhythm" of that time, and it was in sharp contrast to the unmetered music of the Renaissance period.

John Sebastian Bach was the leading composer of the period. He brought Baroque polyphony to its maturity, and the period closes with his death in 1750. Handel was the other great figure in Baroque music. Other important composers include Monteverdi, Purcell, Alessandro Scarlatti, Domenico Scarlatti, Corelli, and Vivaldi.

Summary of Baroque Style

1. Steady rhythm with a modern concept of meters.
2. A firm, solid bass line with figured bass accompaniment.
3. Dynamic levels rather than crescendo and decrescendo, but with no extremes of loud and soft.
4. Major and minor tonalities predominate.

5. Instrumental music tends to feature alternation of solo instruments and strings or groups of instruments.
6. Polyphony predominates.

RELATED RECORDINGS [1]

	AIM	BOL	MSB
Bach			
Badinerie from Suite No. 3 in D Major	III-1		
Air, Gavottes 1 and 2 from Suite No. 3			78040
Bourée, Gigue from Suite No. 3			78041
Fugue in G Minor ("Little")	VI-1		
Gigue from Suite No. 2 in B Minor	I		
"Jesu, Joy of Man's Desiring" from Cantata 147	V-1	62	78316
Corelli-Pinelli			
Suite for Strings: Sarabande, Gigue, Badinerie	VI-2	63	
Handel			
Fireworks Music:			
Bourée	III-2	55	78002
Menuetto	III-2		
Ground, A		53	
Minuet			78318
Water Music: "Hornpipe"	II		78001

THE VIENNESE CLASSICAL PERIOD (1750-1810)

If one had lived in this period, its features would not be as clear to him as they appear to us today, for there were a number of stylistic trends at work. One of these was the *Rococo,* which was in opposition to the grandiose ideas of the Baroque. This style, sometimes called Style Gallant, stressed minute details of ornamentation and sought a delicate elegance on a small scale. The little ceramic figurine as opposed to large and noble statuary seems to typify its spirit. Rococo style abandoned the polyphony of the Baroque in favor of an ornamented homophony. A style trend which appealed to the middle class was called *Empfindsamer Stil* (expressive style); it was most clearly represented by sentimental songs extolling bourgeois virtues. Philosophers emphasized enlightenment—the Age of Reason—and musicians such as Rameau and Beethoven reflected the optimism of the belief that man could ultimately control his environment. Another trend, *Sturm und Drang* (storm and stress) opposed the above ideas and sought philosophical answers in imagination and emotion as opposed to logic and reason, and this emphasis on emotion is believed to be reflected in the music of Haydn, Mozart, and Beethoven. Because cultural life was dominated by the aristocracy, the arts were subservient to the ruling class and became elegant, formalized, restrained, and impersonal. Many composers were employed to serve the aristocratic establishment rather than to serve the churches, as had been common in the past.

Artistic expression with classical characteristics can be found in varying

[1] AIM—*Adventures in Music;* BOL—*Bowmar Orchestral Library;* MSB—*Musical Sound Books.*

degrees in all periods of history. Classical concepts include restraint, clarity, objectivity, symmetry, and conformity. These were the stylistic concepts which dominated the Viennese Classical period. The beat (pulse) was lighter than the more vigorous Baroque pulsation; rhythm patterns were likewise more light and crisp. Tempi were moderate, with ritardando and accelerando coming into more frequent use. The crescendo-decrescendo idea developed in contrast to the dynamic levels of the Baroque style. Repeated phrases or periods were often performed at dynamic levels contrasting with their first appearance, however; a loud phrase would be repeated more softly, and a soft phrase would be repeated more loudly. There was an effect of simplicity and lightness as compared to the heavier features of Baroque music. Polyphony was generally in the background, with clear, straight-forward melodies emphasized. The phrases were likely to be of very regular two- and four-measure lengths. The general design of the music reflected the sophistication of the aristocracy, with form more important than emotion.

The instrumental group at the court of Mannheim, Germany, evolved to form the basis of the modern orchestra, with its sections of strings, woodwinds, brasses, and percussion. The clarinet was introduced. The piano became the favored keyboard instrument rather than the Baroque harpsichord, and instrumental music became more important than vocal music.

Melodies were often folk-like. The concept of melodic *development* became highly important and was skillfully employed. This concerns the utilization of a melody or its motives in many different ways in the fabric of compositions. The texture was thin as compared to that of late Baroque music or of the Romantic period music to follow. Tonality was firmly established. The sonata-allegro form developed; this form is considered one of man's greatest achievements. The symphony, quartet, and concerto evolved to become established forms. Leading composers include Haydn, Mozart, Schubert, Gluck, and Beethoven, whose music bridged the Classical and Romantic periods.

Summary of Classical Style

1. Elegance, grace, and refinement combined with simplicity, serenity, clarity, and restraint.

2. Formal symmetry and balance which result in an impersonal and relatively unemotional style.

3. Homophonic textures with a very clear melodic line.

4. Employment of a variety of dynamics.

5. Ingenious thematic development.

RELATED RECORDINGS

	AIM	BOL	MSB
Gluck			
"Air Gai" from *Iphiginia in Aulis*	I		
Haydn			
Emperor's Hymn (Theme and Variations)			78042
Surprise Symphony:			
Andante (Theme and Variations)		62	78042
Minuet		63	

Mozart
    Menuetto from Divertimento 17 in D   V-2
    Minuet in C   53
    Minuet from Symphony No. 40   62
    Romanza from *Eine kleine Nachtmusik*   IV-1   78004
    Theme from Sonata in A Major   78307

Schubert
    Ballet Music No. 2 from *Rosamunde*   78145
    Symphony No. 5 in B-Flat (First Movement)   V-1

THE ROMANTIC PERIOD (1810-1890)

The aristocratic establishment broke down after the French Revolution, and nineteenth-century liberalism followed. The term "Romantic" is not particularly exact in relation to this period, which contained more cross-currents of philosophical thought than did the Classical period. It was a time of expansion and ferment not unlike the Baroque period in some of its aspects, such as the emergence of a more grandiose style and larger performing groups. When the aristocracy declined, the patronage system in which royalty, nobility, or the church paid composers to write music also declined. This set the composer free to express himself and to hope that the general public—or possibly some wealthy person—would somehow support him in unrestricted artistic endeavors. Thus, while the composer was freed from employer restrictions, he became the victim of economic insecurity, the price he had to pay in order to compose as he pleased. The concert hall became the center of musical activity rather than the palace or the church as in earlier days.

In the general free spirit of the times, rhythm became more free. Syncopation grew in favor, and phrases tended to be less regular than those of the symmetrical music of the Classical period. The moderate tempi of the Classical period were swept away by extremes of fast and slow. *Tempo rubato* [2] reached its full development, and *accelerando* and *ritardando* were used more frequently. Extremes in dynamics were common. Chromaticism and dissonance were increasingly used to give the composer additional means of expression. As the period progressed, harmony became more emphasized as a primary musical element and at the same time came to be less certain about its allegiance to a tonal center. The prevailing texture was thicker and heavier than the clear and light texture of the Classical period. The composer felt unrestricted by older forms and did not permit them to stand in the way of his communication with the listener. While the older forms were modified, there were few new forms other than the tone poem (in which the story dictated the form), the art song, and the rhapsody, a free form. Music for the piano underwent great expansion, moving with mechanical improvements in the instrument.

The music was predominantly homophonic in character, and instrumental melodies were likely to be vocally conceived, as evidenced by the number of them which became popular songs in the twentieth century. The development of harmony which led to the use of tone color as an expressive element was an important aspect. The rise of national schools of composers which attempted to write new music expressive of their particular national culture was a natural result of the "freedom to be different." The music of this period

---

[2] Flexibility of tempo due to slight accelerandos and ritardandos depending upon the performer's or conductor's interpretation of the music.

constitutes the largest part of the music played today and is usually better known by the public than that of any other period. Representative composers include Bizet, Brahms, Chabrier, Chopin, Rimsky-Korsakoff, Mendelssohn, Saint-Saëns, Schumann, Tschaikowsky, Verdi, and Wagner.

Summary of Romantic Style

1. Subjective, descriptive, emotional, and nationalistic elements are characteristic.

2. Instrumental tone color is employed to convey feelings and moods.

3. Expansion in harmonic devices includes such aspects as chromaticism and dissonance.

4. Long, flowing melody lines are prominent and often singable.

5. A wide range of emotional expression is evidenced.

6. There are extremes in both tempo and dynamics.

RELATED RECORDINGS

	AIM	BOL	MSB
Bizet			
Carmen Suite			78136-7
L'Arléssienne Suite No. 2			
Farandole	VI-1		
Minuetto	IV-2		
Brahms			
Hungarian Dance No. 1	V-2		
Hungarian Dance No. 6		62	78110
Liebeslieder Waltzes Nos. 1 to 8			78105
Chabrier			
España Rhapsodie	V-1		
Dvorák			
Slavonic Dance No. 1		55	78111
Slavonic Dance No. 7	IV-2		
Grieg			
Peer Gynt Suite (complete)		59	
"In the Hall of the Mountain King"	III-2		78029
Mahler			
Theme from Third Movement, Symphony No. 1		62	
Mendelssohn			
Scherzo from *A Midsummer Night's Dream*		57	78026
Schumann			
Traumerei from *Scenes from Childhood*	IV-2	63	
Sibelius			
Finlandia		60	
Valse Triste			78108

Tschaikowsky
Nutcracker Suite (complete)   68   78033-4
"Waltz of the Flowers"   IV-1   78035

Wagner
Prelude to Act III of *Lohengrin*   VI-1   78133
"Ride of the Valkyries" from *The Valkyries*   62   78049

THE IMPRESSIONISTIC PERIOD (1890-1910)

While many composers continued to write in the Romantic style, the im-
pressionists reacted against the emotional, descriptive, and texturally heavy
music of the late nineteenth century. Like the impressionist painters and the
symbolist poets of the day, these composers tried to avoid realism in favor of
conveying impressions. The relation between their music and the impressionist
paintings is striking, for both have a hazy and dream-like quality. Nature is
frequently the subject. There is less rhythmic drive and tension present in
this style, and there is a lower dynamic level although the conclusion of some
of the compositions of Ravel would not agree with this. Harmonic experi-
mentation led to attempts to escape the major-minor tonal system by such
means as employing the old modes, the pentatonic and whole-tone scales.
Parallel fourths, fifths, and octaves were favored. Systematic chord progres-
sions of the past were not favored as much as individual chords selected for
their coloristic effects. Blocklike chords were arranged in parallel motion, and
there were "escaped chords" which did not resolve, but seemed to "escape" to
distant and indistinct tonalities. Tone color was raised to equal status with
harmony while melody declined in importance. This musical style can be
viewed as a transition from nineteenth-century music to the Contemporary
period which follows.

Instruments were employed in new ways; for example, the very low register
of the flute was exploited, as was the very high register of the trombone.
Mutes were used and the harp was favored; both of these contributed to tone
color and special effects. Leading composers included Debussy, Ravel, Delius,
Griffes, de Falla, and Respighi.

Summary of Impressionistic Style

1. Melodies tend to be vague; at times they seem to be only remnants of the long
   and flowing Romantic melodies. Thematic development is almost absent.

2. The tone color is misty, blurred, and pastel in effect. Muted instruments and
   employment of extreme ranges of instruments contribute to this tone color.

3. The harmony is often unexpected, unresolved, and yields a vague fairylike
   atmosphere. A trend away from the major-minor system is evident.

4. The texture is luminous and transparent.

5. The form is often simple, sometimes a series of episodes.

	AIM	BOL	MSB
Debussy			
Children's Corner: (complete)		62	78036-7
"Snow Is Dancing"	III-1		78037
"Play of the Waves" from *La Mer*	VI-2		
de Falla			
Spanish Dance No. 1 from *La Vida Breve*	VI-1		
Griffes			
The White Peacock	VI-1		
Ravel			
Mother Goose Suite:			
Laideronette (Empress of the Pagoda)	IV-2	57	78013
Beauty and the Beast	V-1	57	78014
Respighi			
Villa Borghese from *Pines of Rome*	IV-1		78127

THE CONTEMPORARY PERIOD (1910-   )

The most difficult period to analyze is the one in which we live; there has not been sufficient lapse of time to be able to "see the forest for the trees." However, certain generalizations can be made. We have seen the gradual abandonment of the major-minor tonality which began in the late nineteenth century become an actuality in the Contemporary period. While some composers of stature continue to utilize traditional harmony, many others have found it to be inadequate for them. In its place we find some of the music constructed on arbitrary "tone rows" which avoid any reference to major and minor scales. The old modes are sometimes utilized, as are Oriental scales and some heretofore overlooked scales found in folk music of some Western countries. Dissonance has been employed to such an extent as to blur the distinction formerly existing between it and consonance. Some composers experiment with microtones, scale steps smaller than the traditional half step. Polytonality combines two or more keys (tonalities); polyrhythm combines two or more rhythms or meters. Polyphony again interests composers, and the old techniques of the past are revived in new harmonic settings which are often dissonant. Chords are constructed as composers choose to build them, and it is common to find them as a series of fourths or fifths rather than as a series of thirds that was a cornerstone of the old harmony. Some Classical trends can be seen, such as objectivity (less emotionalism) and a thin, clear texture. Rhythm has become much more complex with what might be a partial return toward the unmeasured and unmetered music of the Renaissance period. There is often a strong rhythmic drive, a great deal of tension, and a mechanical aspect of style which opposes the Romantic rubato style of the nineteenth century. Unorthodox instrumental combinations remind the listener of those of the Baroque period.

The freedom of the composers to compose as they please seems to be complete. They no longer rely on the church, the aristocracy, or on wealthy patrons. Most composers of today are employed as college teachers, librarians and in other occupations; they are seldom employed as composers. Thus, most of them are free to compose whatever they like in a manner somewhat similar to the scientist in a laboratory who does pure research. For example, one of the most advanced composers of his day was Charles Ives, who made his living in insurance and composed the music he wanted to compose after his day's work was done. The best of these composers have mastered the styles and techniques of the music of the past so that they can draw upon all of these resources in the creation of the "new music." Added to these are new resources of this century which include musical instruments such as those invented by Harry Partch, and electronic music which utilizes sounds placed on tape and sounds programed through computers. Composers include Bartók, Ginastera, Kodaly, Villa-Lobos, Shostakovitch, Stravinsky, Schoenberg, Ives, Schuller, Stockhausen, and many more.

Summary of Contemporary Style

1. A mixture of styles is to be found.

2. A strong trend toward avoiding traditional major-minor tonality is evident.

3. The texture is likely to be thin.

4. Melodies are often fragmentary and angular; they tend to be instrumentally conceived.

5. Dissonance is emphasized in both harmony and counterpoint.

6. Bitonality and polytonality (two or more keys at once) are often employed.

7. The rhythm tends to be irregular, energetic, and insistent; it may be poly-rhythmic.

8. The style is experimental, unemotional, and impersonal.

RELATED RECORDINGS

	AIM	BOL	MSB
Bartók			
Hungarian Sketches:			
"Bear Dance"	III-2		
"Evening in the Village"	V-2		
Copland			
"Circus Music" from *Red Pony* Suite	III-1		
"Hoe-Down" from *Rodeo*	V-2	55	
"Simple Gifts" from *Appalachian Spring*		65	78152
Ginastera			
"Wheat Dance" from *Estancia Ballet* Suite	IV-1		

Some examples should be sought from other sources such as Folkways FT 3612, "Twelve-Tone Music" and Folkways FX 6160, "Sounds of New Music" which includes Cowell's tone clusters, Cage's prepared piano, Varése's isolation of rhythm, electronic music, and multiple tape music.

14

Instruments and Voices

In the preceding chapter there were references made to the evolution of instrumental music which culminated in the large nineteenth-century orchestra. In this evolution two influences reacted upon one another: the trends in musical styles and the mechanical improvement of the instruments. The instruments of the orchestra are capable of producing a stunning array of tone colors and fascinating gradations of dynamics, pitch, and tone quality. As complex as all this is, the musical capabilities rest upon a number of simple scientific facts. Sound is produced by vibration. The faster the vibration, the higher the pitch; the slower the vibration, the lower the pitch. The quality of sound is affected by the materials from which the instrument is constructed, the shape of resonating chambers, and the manner in which the sound is produced.

The symphony orchestra is comprised of four sections: the strings, the woodwinds, the brasses, and the percussion. Even a rudimentary knowledge of instruments which comprise these sections will enhance your enjoyment in listening to instrumental music.

THE STRINGS

The instruments of the violin family and the harp comprise this section. The members of the violin family look alike except for their size. The smallest is the violin; the viola is slightly larger. Both are held up with the left hand and bowed with the right. The cello is sufficiently large so that it must rest on the floor with the player sitting down to play it. Largest is the double bass (string bass); the player either stands up to play it or he sits on a high stool.

The string sound is made by bowing or plucking the strings, causing them to vibrate. The bow is made of coarse hair mounted on a wooden frame. Rosin is placed on the hair and this substance causes the friction which makes the strings vibrate. Thin, short strings produce high sounds, and long, thicker strings produce lower sounds. The player's fingers have the effect of shortening or lengthening the vibrating parts of the strings, thus producing different pitches.

The harp has forty-three strings and seven pedals which are used to adjust the strings to the proper keys needed. The harp's strings are stroked or plucked to produce the sound. The player sits on a chair to play this large instrument.

THE STRINGS: (A) violin, (B) viola, (C) cello, (D) string bass.

THE WOODWINDS: (A) flute, (B) piccolo, (C) bass clarinet, (D) clarinet, (E) saxophone, (F) bassoon, (G) contra bassoon, (H) oboe, (I) English horn.

Photographs courtesy of Bowmar Records, Inc.

THE BRASSES: (A) trumpet, (B) French horn,
(C) tuba, (D) trombone.

PERCUSSION INSTRUMENTS: (A) chimes, (B) glockenspiel, (C) celeste, (D) xylophone,
(E) glockenspiel, (F) temple blocks, (G) tympani, (H) snare drum, (I) bass drum,
(J) gong, (K) maracas, (L) castanets, (M) triangle, (N) cymbals, (O) tambourine,
(P) wood block.

Photographs courtesy of Bowmar Records, Inc.

THE WOODWINDS

The piccolo and flute are played by blowing across a mouth-hole to produce what is called an "edge tone." The air is directed to the edge of the hole by the lips. The piccolo is the highest-pitched instrument of the woodwinds, as might be expected from its tiny size. The flute is twice the length of the piccolo, thus it is pitched one octave lower. The oboe, English horn, bassoon, and contra bassoon are played with double reeds, while the clarinets and saxophones are played with single reeds. The contra bassoon sounds the lowest pitches of any instrument in the orchestra. Both the clarinet and saxophone are members of the same family and there are different sizes of each instrument. The saxophone is more popular in the band than it is in the orchestra, but it is used in the orchestra occasionally. While saxophones and most flutes and piccolos are not made of wood, they are still classified as woodwind instruments.

THE BRASSES

The brass instrument player produces sound by vibrating his lips against a cupped mouthpiece. The valves on the trumpet, French horn, and tuba detour the vibrating air column into shorter and longer tubing to raise or lower the pitch. Another influence on pitch production is the degree of tension or relaxation in the player's lips; the greater the tension, the higher the pitch. The trumpet is the highest pitched brass instrument and the tuba is the lowest. The trombones have no valves. Their slides accomplish the same purpose as valves on the other brasses by shortening or lengthening the vibrating air column. Some brass instruments such as the baritone and melophone are used exclusively in bands. The Sousaphone is a type of tuba designed for the marching band.

THE PERCUSSION

Vibrations which produce sound from percussion instruments are set in motion by striking. There are three classifications of percussion instruments: those on which a membrane is struck, those which are solid, and those which are of the keyboard type. The keyboard type instruments and the tympani have definite pitch; the others do not. The percussion section also includes a number of special effect devices, from bird whistles to anvils, too numerous to mention.

Membrane	Solid	Keyboard
bongo drums	castanets	celeste
conga drums	claves	chimes
bass drum	cymbals	orchestra bells
snare drum	gong	(glockenspiel)
tambourine	maracas	marimba
tympani	triangle	piano
(kettledrums)	wood block	xylophone

216

Courtesy The New York Philharmonic Society.

217

OVERTURE

to *Die Meistersinger von Nürnberg*, Excerpt

Wagner

218

(Wagner: Overture to *Die Meistersinger von Nurnberg*, Excerpt) of Hardy and Fish's *A Workbook for Analysis—Music Literature, Volume I: Homophony*

As wonderful as the modern instruments are, there is no instrument which can equal the appeal of singing voices. Voices, with their imperfections, are after all, *human,* while the instruments are at best artistic tools to use.

Voices are classified in accordance with their range and quality. The most broad classifications are simply soprano and alto for women and tenor and bass for men. There are, however, a number of subdivisions of these classes, as shown below.

Approximate Vocal Ranges

The above average ranges do not depict the true range of many of the voices described below which may exceed the approximate ranges by wide margins.

Adult Voice Classifications

Coloratura Soprano: The highest range; a very agile voice.

Lyric Soprano: Light, high voice, not as agile as coloratura.

Dramatic Soprano: A heavier voice with more theatrical quality.

Mezzo Soprano: Darker quality of tone; rich low range.

Contralto: The lowest female voice; somewhat heavy in quality.

Lyric Tenor: Highest male voice, very light in quality.

Dramatic Tenor: A heavier tenor voice with more theatrical quality. Sometimes called "Tenor Robusto."

Baritone: Has range of a bass, but quality reminiscent of tenor.

Bass: The lowest male voice; an exceptionally low voice is sometimes called "Basso Profundo."

RECORDINGS FOR STUDY

Instruments

Bowmar Records	*Meet the Instruments* (Filmstrips and pictures available)
Capitol Records	*Instruments of the Orchestra* (Narration by Yehudi Menuhin)
Decca Records	*The Symphony Orchestra*
Folkways	*The Orchestra and Its Instruments*
Jam Handy	*Instruments of the Symphony Orchestra* (Filmstrips available)
RCA Victor Co.	*Instruments of the Orchestra* (Pictures available)
Vanguard	*Instruments of the Orchestra* (Narration by David Randolph)

Voices

Coloratura Soprano	Delibes: "Bell Song" from *Lakmé*
	Handel: "Rejoice Greatly" from *Messiah*
Lyric Soprano	Handel: "Come Unto Him" from *Messiah*
	Villa-Lobos: *Bachianas Brasilieras No. 5*
Dramatic Soprano	Mozart: "Dove sono" from *The Marriage of Figaro*
	Wagner: "Dich, Teure Halle" from *Tannhäuser*
Mezzo Soprano	Bizet: "Habanera" from *Carmen*
	Offenbach: "Barcarolle" from *Tales of Hoffmann*
Contralto	Bach: "Herzliebster Jesu" from *St. Matthew Passion*
	Handel: "He Was Despised" from *Messiah*
Lyric Tenor	Handel: "Every Valley" from *Messiah*
	Rimsky-Korsakoff: "Song of India" from *Sadko*
Baritone	Bizet: "Toreador Song" from *Carmen*
	Handel: "Where E'er You Walk" from *Semele*
Bass	Handel: "Why Do the Nations" from *Messiah*
	Moussorgsky: "Farewell of Boris" from *Boris Godunov*

Appendix A

do

ti

la

so

fa

mi

re

do

222

Appendix B

Some Common Musical Terms

TERM	MEANING
Accelerando (accel.)	Gradually increasing the speed
Adagio	Slowly, leisurely
Allegretto	Moderately fast, slower than allegro
Allegro	Lively, brisk, rapid
Andante	Moderately slow
Animato	With animation
A tempo	In the original tempo
Con	With
Con moto	With motion
Con spirito	With spirit
Coda	A supplement at end of composition
Crescendo (cresc.)	Increasing in loudness
Da Capo (D. C.)	From the beginning
Dal Segno (D. S.)	From the sign
Decrescendo (decresc.)	Decreasing in loudness
Diminuendo (dim.)	Gradually softer
Dolce (dol.)	Softly, sweetly
Espressivo	With expression
Fermata	Hold (prolong)
Fine	The end
Forte (f)	Loud
Forte-piano (fp)	Accent strongly, diminishing
Fortissimo (ff)	Very loud
Grandioso	Grand, pompous, majestic
Grave	Very slow
Largo	Broad and slow
Legato	Smoothly, the reverse of staccato
Lento	Slow, between andante and largo
Maestoso	Majestically, dignified
Mezzo-piano (mp)	Moderately soft
Moderato	Moderately

Pianissimo (pp)	Very softly
Piano (p)	Softly
Presto	Very quick
Rallentando (rall.)	Gradually slower
Ritardando (rit.)	Gradually slower and slower
Ritenuto	In slower time
Sforzando (sf)	Forcibly, with sudden emphasis
Sostenuto	Sustained, prolonged
Staccato	Detached, separate
Tempo	Movement, rate of speed
Tranquillo	Quietly
Troppo	Much
Un poco	A little
Vivace	Bright, spirited
Vivo	Lively, spirited

Appendix C

Patriotic Songs

AMERICA

Samuel Francis Smith

Henry Carey (?)

THE STAR-SPANGLED BANNER
(SERVICE VERSION)

Francis Scott Key

John Stafford Smith

With spirit (♩ = 104)

1. O___ say! can you see,___ by the dawn's ear - ly light,
2. On the shore, dim - ly seen___ thru the mists of the deep,
3. O___ thus be it ev - er when___ free men shall stand

What so proud - ly we hailed at the twi - light's last gleam - ing?
Where the foe's haught - y host in dread si - lence re - pos - es,
Be - tween their lov'd homes and the war's des - o - la - tion!

Whose broad stripes and bright stars, thru the per - il - ous fight,
What is that which the breeze, o'er the tow - er - ing steep,
Blest with vic - t'ry and peace, may the heav'n - res - cued land

O'er the ram - parts we watch'd, were so gal - lant - ly stream - ing?
As it fit - ful - ly blows, half con - ceals, half dis - clos - es?
Praise the Pow'r that hath made and pre - served us a na - tion!

And the rock-ets' red glare, the bombs burst-ing in air,
Now it catch-es the gleam of the morn-ing's first beam,
Then con-quer we must, when our cause it is just,

Gave proof thru the night that our flag was still there.
In full glo-ry re-flect-ed now shines on the stream;
And this be our mot-to: "In God is our trust!"

CHORUS

O say, does that Star-Span-gled Ban-ner yet wave
'Tis the star Span-gled Ban-ner, O long may it wave
And the star Span-gled Ban-ner in tri-umph shall wave

broaden

O'er the land of the free and the home of the brave?
O'er the land of the free and the home of the brave!
O'er the land of the free and the home of the brave!

227

AMERICA THE BEAUTIFUL

Katherine Lee Bates

Samuel A. Ward

1. O beau-ti-ful for spa-cious skies, For am-ber waves of grain,___
2. O beau-ti-ful for pil-grim feet Whose stern im-pas-sion'd stress___
3. O beau-ti-ful for he-roes prov'd In lib-er-at-ing strife,___
4. O beau-ti-ful for pa-triot dream That sees be-yond the years.___

For pur-ple moun-tain maj-es-ties A-bove the fruit-ed plain.___
A thor-ough fare for free-dom beat A cross the wil-der-ness.___
Who more than self their coun-try loved, And mer-cy more than life.___
Thine al-a-bas ter cit-ies gleam Un-dimmed by hu-man tears.___

A-mer-i-ca! A-mer-i-ca! God shed His grace on thee,___
A-mer-i-ca! A-mer-i-ca! God mend thine ev-'ry flaw,___
A-mer-i-ca! A-mer-i-ca! May God thy gold re-fine___
A-mer-i-ca! A-mer-i-ca! God shed His grace on thee,___

And crown thy good with broth-er-hood From sea to shin-ing sea.
Con-firm thy soul in self con-trol, Thy lib-er-ty in law.
Till all suc-cess be no ble-ness, And ev-'ry gain di-vine.
And crown thy good with broth-er-hood From sea to shin-ing sea.

Indices

Index of Songs

Index of Instrumental Compositions

Index